BEANIES &
BOBBLE HATS

BEANIES &
BOBBLE HATS

36 QUICK AND STYLISH KNITS

FIONA GOBLE

CICO BOOKS
LONDON NEW YORK

To my sister Louise for all her help and knitting companionship

Published in 2015 by CICO Books
An imprint of Ryland Peters & Small Ltd
20–21 Jockey's Fields
London WC1R 4BW
341 E 116th St
New York, NY 10029

www.rylandpeters.com

10 9 8 7 6 5 4 3 2 1

Text © Fiona Goble 2015
Design and photography
© CICO Books 2015

A CIP catalog record for this book is
available from the Library of Congress
and the British Library.

ISBN: 978 1 78249 196 5

Printed in China

Editor: Kate Haxell
Designer: Vicky Rankin
Photographer: Terry Benson
**Stylist and Photographic
Art Direction:** Luis Peral
Hair and make-up: Carol Morley and
Lidio Netto

In-house designer: Fahema Khanam
Art director: Sally Powell
Production director: Patricia Harrington
Publishing manager: Penny Craig
Publisher: Cindy Richards

Contents

Introduction

These days, knitted hats aren't just for winter. They're a must-have item to put the finishing touch to everyday outfits—whether you're strolling through the countryside or on your usual brisk walk to work. Pull your hat down at the back for a nonchalant look, or roll it down over your ears when the weather gets serious—the decision is yours.

One of the loveliest things about creating hats is that they're a great way to perfect your skills and try out new stitch combinations, without committing yourself to having to knit every evening for months on end to finish the project. And because you only need a ball or two of yarn for each one, you can whip up a great selection of berets and beanies for family and friends—and yourself, of course—without spending too much.

This collection of hats includes styles for women and men of all ages and tastes, and there's a great collection for children, too. Choose from sassy bobble berets, Nordic-inspired two-color knits, or the classic head-hugging beanie. And if you want a go-to choice for those days when the temperatures haven't plummeted too low, why not give one of the ear-warming headbands a go?

Lots of the styles in this book are suitable for beginners with just a couple of projects under their belt, and all the hats are well within the grasp of the "advanced beginner" or intermediate knitter. If you've mastered the knitting basics and know how to decrease, there's a great range of designs to choose from. And if you feel like a bit of a challenge, why not give some simple Fair Isle a go, or get to grips with cables? I can guarantee both are a lot easier than you might think.

Almost all the yarns in this book come in a great range of colors, so have a browse through your local or online yarn store to find a shade to fall in love with. You can substitute a yarn that I've used for another yarn of the same type, but please see the notes on yarn substitution on page 115, and make sure you buy enough yarn to complete your project. If you are knitting with a different yarn, it is also extra important to knit a gauge square before you begin (see page 116), to make sure your finished hat will be the right size.

I've loved creating the hats in this book and I hope you'll love knitting them every bit as much.

Knits

From slouchy beanies with seriously simple shaping, to color and texture patterns that make a major statement, there are projects in this book for novice and master knitters alike.

Fair Isle bobble hat
instructions on page 78

**Big and little
stripes beanie**
instructions on page 79

Two-color lacy beanie
instructions on page 80

Pixie pompom hat
instructions on page 81

16

Fairytale hood
instructions on page 82

"A hat that's not too serious..."

Stitch-pattern slouchy beanie

**Stitch-pattern
slouchy beanie**
instructions on page 83

**Bobble beanie
with earflaps**
instructions on page 84

Zigzag bobble hat
instructions on page 85

"*Multicolored yarn is a godsend…*"

"When it's not quite cold enough for a hat..."

**Chunky headband
two ways**
instructions on page 87

**Simple knit
bobble hat**
instructions on page 88

Tweedy two-tone beanie
instructions on page 89

Lacy panels beanie
instructions on page 90

Fancy rib slouchy beanie

**Fancy rib
slouchy beanie**

instructions on page 91

Self-striped slouchy beanie
instructions on page 92

**Lacy cloche
with flower**
instructions on page 93

"Don't worry, the stitch pattern's very easy…"

Retro bobble hat
instructions on page 96

Cable-band beret
instructions on page 97

Simple sideways beanie
instructions on page 98

Cable beret
instructions on page 99

Slouchy beanie with buttons
instructions on page 100

Diagonals beret
instructions on page 101

Cabled slouchy beanie
instructions on page 102

Button-trim beret
instructions on page 103

Cable rib beanie
instructions on page 104

Peaked newsboy beret
instructions on page 105

Turban-style beanie
instructions on page 106

Three-color bobble hat
instructions on page 107

Fair Isle border beanie
instructions on page 108

"Something with panache to show off your knitting skills..."

Pumpkin beanie
instructions on page 109

"A good-enough-to-eat pumpkin hat…"

Heart beanie
instructions on page 110

"Because you love to knit…"

69

Tricolor bobble hat
instructions on page 111

Bow beanie
instructions on page 112

Knitted crown
instructions on page 113

"Turn the child in your life into a prince or princess…"

Knitted crown   75

Patterns

On the following pages you'll find the knitting patterns for all of the hats. The knitting needles, yarn, and other items that you need are listed at the beginning of each pattern.

FAIR ISLE BOBBLE HAT

A serious contender for my favorite hat in the whole book, this Nordic-look bobble hat takes its inspiration from the sort of hats that were fashionable on the ski slopes in 1970-something. We knew a thing or two about fashion way back when. If you're new to Fair Isle knitting, this is the perfect place to start, because the color changes are very close together so there's no stranding involved.

Yarn
Sublime Baby Cashmere Merino Silk DK (75% wool, 20% silk, 5% cashmere) light worsted (DK) yarn
1 x 1¾oz (50g) ball (127yd/116m) in shade 192 Teddy Red (A)
1 x 1¾oz (50g) ball (127yd/116m) in shade 344 Little Linen (B)

Needles and equipment
US 6 (4mm) knitting needles
Yarn sewing needle
A pompom maker to make 2¾in (7cm) pompoms, or two cardboard circles each measuring 2¾in (7cm) in diameter with a 1¼in (3cm) diameter hole in the center.

Gauge (tension)
22 sts and 28 rows in stockinette (stocking) stitch to a 4-in (10-cm) square on US 6 (4mm) needles.

Measurements
The finished hat measures approx. 16in (40cm) circumference and 8½in (22cm) high.

Abbreviations
See page 126.

For the hat
Cast on 102 sts in A.
Row 1: [K1, p1] to end.
Rep row 1, 11 times more.
Break A and join in B.
Work 14 rows from chart.
Rep last 14 rows once more.
Rep rows 1–10 of the chart once.
Cont in B only.

Row 51: K1, [skpo, k5] to last 3 sts, skpo, k1. *(87 sts)*
Row 52: Purl.
Row 53: K3, [sl2, k1, p2sso, k3] to end. *(59 sts)*
Row 54: P1, [p2tog] to end. *(30 sts)*
Row 55: [K2tog] to end. *(15 sts)*
Row 56: [P2tog] 3 times, p3tog, [p2tog] 3 times. *(7 sts)*
Break yarn, thread it through rem sts, and pull up securely.

To make up
Sew the back seam using mattress stitch (see page 124).
Using the pompom maker or cardboard circles, make a pompom, winding yarns A and B together. Tie the pompom using B. Trim the pompom and use the tails of yarn to sew it to the top of the hat.
Weave in all loose ends.

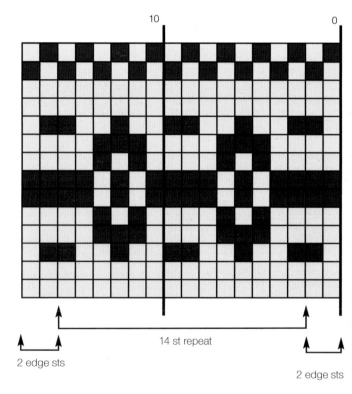

10   0

14 st repeat

2 edge sts

2 edge sts

key

Teddy Red (A) ■

Little Linen (B) □

BIG AND LITTLE STRIPES BEANIE

Everyone loves a timeless beanie classic—and this one is a dream to make, even for newbie knitters. I've used a soft, light worsted (DK) yarn with a dash of super-soft cashmere—but the pattern would work well in most yarns of this weight, and could be a great yarn stash-buster. Knit it in two colors as I have, or make it plain. Use gentle combinations, or make yourself some dashing rainbow stripes. Rifle through your knitting basket or the shelves of your local yarn store, see what's on offer—and have some fun.

Yarn
Sublime Baby Cashmere Merino Silk DK (75% extra fine merino, 20% silk, 5% cashmere) light worsted (DK) yarn
1 x 1¾oz (50g) ball (127yd/116m) in shade 277 Tittlemouse (A)
1 x 1¾oz (50g) ball (127yd/116m) in shade 357 Tiffany (B)

Needles and equipment
US 6 (4mm) knitting needles
Yarn sewing needle

Gauge (tension)
22 sts and 28 rows in stockinette (stocking) stitch to a 4-in (10-cm) square on US 6 (4mm) needles.

Measurements
The finished hat measures approx. 13½in (34cm) circumference and 10¼in (26cm) high.

Abbreviations
See page 126.

For the hat
Cast on 96 sts in A.
Row 1: [K2, p2] to end.
Rep row 1, 15 times more.
Break A and join in B.
Rep row 1, 10 times more.
Leave B at side and join in A.
Rep row 1, 4 times more.
Break A and use B.
Rep row 1, 20 times more.
Break B and work rem of hat in A.
Rep row 1, 14 times more.

Row 65: [K2, p2tog] to end. *(72 sts)*
Row 66: [K1, p2] to end.
Row 67: [Skpo, p1] to end. *(48 sts)*
Row 68: [K2, p1] to end.
Row 69: [Sl1 kwise, p1, psso] to end. *(24 sts)*
Row 70: [P2tog] to end. *(12 sts)*
Break yarn, thread it through rem sts, and pull up securely.

To make up
Sew the back seam using flat stitch (see page 125).
Weave in all loose ends.

TWO-COLOR LACY BEANIE

On a chilly and miserable day I think there's something comforting about pulling on a colorful hat in a nice fuzzy yarn. If you have that feeling, too, then this could be the perfect hat for you. It's a lacy stitch—but please don't be afraid of it. Lacy stitches are so much easier than they look—just remember to take it slowly at first. Once you've done the first pattern repeat, you'll probably find it so satisfying you won't want to knit anything too plain again.

Yarn

Bergere de France Plume (47% polyamide, 42% acrylic, 11% wool) chunky yarn
1 x 1¾oz (50g) ball (65yd/60m) in shade 25525 Rosat (A)
1 x 1¾oz (50g) ball (65yd/60m) in shade 24768 Aureole (B)

Needles and equipment

US 8 (5mm) knitting needles
US 9 (5.5mm) knitting needles
Yarn sewing needle

Gauge (tension)

15 sts and 20 rows in stockinette (stocking) stitch to a 4-in (10-cm) square on US 9 (5.5mm) needles.

Measurements

The finished hat measures approx. 17½in (44cm) circumference and 8½in (22cm) high.

Abbreviations

See page 126.

For the hat

Using US 8 (5mm) needles and A, cast on 79 sts.
Row 1: [K1, p1] to last st, k1.
Row 2: [P1, k1] to last st, p1.
Rep rows 1–2 twice more.
Break A, join in B and change to US 9 (5.5mm) needles.
Row 7: [K1, k2tog, yo, k1, yo, k2togtbl] to last st, k1.
Row 8: Purl.
Row 9: K2tog, [yo, k3, yo, sl2, k1, p2sso] to last 5 sts, yo, k3, yo, k2togtbl.
Row 10: Purl.
Row 11: [K1, yo, k2togtbl, k1, k2tog, yo] to last st, k1.

Row 12: Purl.
Row 13: K2, [yo, sl2, k1, p2sso, yo, k3] to last 5 sts, yo, sl2, k1, p2sso, yo, k2.
Row 14: Purl.
Rep rows 7–14, 3 times more.
Row 33: K2, [sk2po, k3] to last 5 sts, sk2po, k2. *(53 sts)*
Row 34: Purl.
Row 35: [K2tog] to last st, k1. *(27 sts)*
Row 36: [K2tog] 6 times, k3, [k2tog] 6 times. *(15 sts)*
Row 37: [K2tog] 3 times, sk2po, [k2tog] 3 times. *(7 sts)*
Break yarn, thread it through rem sts, and pull up securely.

To make up

Sew the back seam using flat stitch (see page 125).
Weave in all loose ends.

PIXIE POMPOM HAT

This super-chunky knit, pointy bobble hat is ideal for newbie knitters who want their project to grow at a cracking pace—without sacrificing style, of course. The yarn is beautifully soft and warm and the hat's generous size means you can pull it right down over your ears when the wind—or even the snow—is whooshing round your head. So why are you sitting there waiting? Grab your needles and yarn and get started.

Yarn

Sirdar Big Softie (51% wool, 49% acrylic) super-chunky yarn
2 x 1¾oz (50g) balls (49yd/45m) in shade 321 Beanie (A)
1 x 1¾oz (50g) ball (49yd/45m) in shade 330 Meringue (B)

Needles and equipment

US 13 (9mm) knitting needles
US 15 (10mm) knitting needles
Yarn sewing needle
A pompom maker to make 4½in (11.5cm) pompoms, or two cardboard circles each measuring 4½in (11.5cm) in diameter with a 2¼in (5.5cm) diameter hole in the center.

Gauge (tension)

9 sts and 12 rows in stockinette (stocking) stitch to a 4-in (10-cm) square on US 15 (10mm) needles.

Measurements

The finished hat measures approx. 20in (50cm) circumference and 21½in (55cm) high, excluding pompom.

Abbreviations

See page 126.

For the hat

Using US 13 (9mm) needles, cast on 52 sts in A.
Leave A at side and join in B.
Row 1: [K2, p2] to end.
Row 2: [K2, p2] to end.
Leave B at side and use A.
Row 3: [K2, p2] to end.
Row 4: [K2, p2] to end.
Leave A at side and use B.
Row 5: [K2, p2] to end.
Row 6: [K2, p2] to end.
Break B, change to US 15 (10mm) needles and work remainder of hat in A.
Beg with a k row, work 14 rows in st st.
Row 21: K5, [k2tog, k8] 4 times, k2tog, k5. *(47 sts)*
Beg with a p row, work 5 rows in st st.
Row 27: K4, [k2tog, k7] twice, sl2, k1, p2sso, [k7, k2tog] twice, k4. *(41 sts)*
Beg with a p row, work 5 rows in st st.

Row 33: K3, [k2tog, k6] twice, sl2, k1, p2sso, [k6, k2tog] twice, k3. *(35 sts)*
Beg with a p row, work 5 rows in st st.
Row 39: K2, [k2tog, k5] twice, sl2, k1, p2sso, [k5, k2tog] twice, k2. *(29 sts)*
Beg with a p row, work 5 rows in st st.
Row 45: K1, [k2tog, k4] twice, sl2, k1, p2sso, [k4, k2tog] twice, k1. *(23 sts)*
Beg with a p row, work 3 rows in st st.
Row 49: [K2tog, k3] twice, sl2, k1, p2sso, [k3, k2tog] twice. *(17 sts)*
Beg with a p row, work 3 rows in st st.
Row 53: K2tog, k1, k2tog, k2, sl2, k1, p2sso, k2, k2tog, k1, k2tog. *(11 sts)*
Beg with a p row, work 3 rows in st st.
Row 57: [K2tog, k1] 3 times, k2tog. *(7 sts)*
Row 58: Purl.
Row 59: K2tog, sl2, k1, p2sso, k2tog. *(3 sts)*
Break yarn, thread it through rem sts, and pull up securely.

To make up

Sew the back seam using flat stitch (see page 125).
Using the pompom maker or cardboard circles, make a large pompom in B. Trim the pompom and use the tails of yarn to sew it to the top of the hat.
Weave in all loose ends.

FAIRYTALE HOOD

*Cozy up in your own little world
under this soft and comfy hood. It's
knitted on really big needles so will
be quick to finish, even for a novice
knitter. The main part of the hood is
knitted in a light-as-a-feather alpaca-
mix yarn, which comes in a range
of dazzling jewel shades and gentle
neutrals. I've finished the lower
edge of the hood with a crochet
trim: it's really simple to do, and
I'll show you exactly how. But if
you prefer your hat crochet-free,
then that's all right, too.*

Yarn
Sirdar Big Softie (51% wool,
49% acrylic) super-chunky yarn
1 x 1¾oz (50g) ball (49yd/45m) in
shade 330 Meringue (A)
Rowan Tumble (90% alpaca,
10% cotton) super-chunky yarn
1 x 3½oz (100g) ball (77yd/70m) in
shade 566 Sky (B)

Needles and equipment
US 17 (12mm) knitting needles
US L-11 (8mm) or similar size crochet
hook (optional)

Gauge (tension)
8 sts and 11 rows in stockinette
(stocking) stitch to a 4-in (10-cm)
square on US 17 (12mm) needles.

Measurements
The back seam of the finished hood
measures approx. 9½in (24cm) and the
hood measures approx. 10¼in (26cm)
from the front edge to the back seam.

Abbreviations
See page 126.

For the hat
Cast on 44 sts in A.
Break A and join in B.
Knit 2 rows.
Beg with a k row, work 14 rows in st st.
Row 17: K2, k2tog, k to last 4 sts, ssk,
k2. *(42 sts)*
Row 18: Purl.
Rep rows 17–18, 4 times more. *(34 sts)*
Bind (cast) off.

To make up
Sew the back seam using
mattress stitch (see page 124).
Using the crochet hook, work
crochet edging (see page 125)
along the back edge of the
hood using yarn A.
To make each of the two
tassels, cut 24 x 14-in (36-cm)
lengths of A and two
9-in (23-cm) lengths of yarn.
Lay the longer lengths in a
neat bunch. Tie one of the
shorter lengths of yarn tightly
around the center of the bunch.
Fold the ends of the lengths
downward and tie the second
short length of yarn tightly
around the bunch of the yarn,
about 1½in (4cm) from the
center tie, to form the tassel.
Trim the tassels and secure
them to the corners of the hood.
Weave in all loose ends.

STITCH-PATTERN SLOUCHY BEANIE

I've given this texture-stripe beanie a subtle twist by adding a super-soft alpaca border with a little turned-up edge. The main part of the hat is a tad more classic—and is perfect for cool mornings and evenings that sometimes call for a hat—but not one that's too serious.

Yarn
Rowan Alpaca Color (100% alpaca) light worsted (DK) yarn
1 x 1¾oz (50g) ball (131yd/120m) in shade 138 Ruby (A)
Cascade 220 Superwash (100% wool) worsted (Aran) yarn
1 x 3½oz (100g) ball (220yd/200m) in shade 1940 Peach (B)

Needles and equipment
US 5 (3.75mm) knitting needles
US 6 (4mm) knitting needles
Yarn sewing needle

Gauge (tension)
22 sts and 30 rows in stockinette (stocking) stitch to a 4-in (10-cm) square on US 6 (4mm) needles.

Measurements
The finished hat measures approx. 17in (44cm) circumference and 9½in (24cm) high.

Abbreviations
See page 126.

For the hat
Using US 5 (3.75mm) needles, cast on 102 sts in A.
Beg with a k row, work 4 rows in st st.
Row 5: K2, [p2, k2] to end.
Row 6: P2, [k2, p2] to end.
Rows 7–10: Rep rows 5–6 twice more.
Break A, join in B and change to US 6 (4mm) needles.
Beg with a k row, work 6 rows in st st.
Beg with a p row, work 6 rows in st st.
Rep last 12 rows, 3 times more.
Beg with a k row, work 2 rows in st st.
Row 61: K7, [sk2po, k14] 5 times, sk2po, k7. *(90 sts)*
Row 62: Purl.
Row 63: K6, [sk2po, k12] 5 times, sk2po, k6. *(78 sts)*
Row 64: Purl.
Row 65: K5, [sk2po, k10] 5 times, sk2po, k5. *(66 sts)*
Row 66: Purl.
Row 67: K4, [sk2po, k8] 5 times, sk2po, k4. *(54 sts)*

Row 68: Purl.
Row 69: K3, [sk2po, k6] 5 times, sk2po, k3. *(42 sts)*
Row 70: Purl.
Row 71: K2, [sk2po, k4] 5 times, sk2po, k2. *(30 sts)*
Row 72: Purl.
Row 73: K1, [sk2po, k2] 5 times, sk2po, k1. *(18 sts)*
Row 74: [P2tog] to end. *(9 sts)*
Break yarn, thread it through rem sts, and pull up securely.

To make up
Sew the back seam using mattress stitch (see page 124).
Weave in all loose ends.

BOBBLE BEANIE WITH EARFLAPS

*On those freezing cold days
when the wind is swirling around
your head, a hat with earflaps is
borderline vital. With this beanie,
you won't have to pull it down so far
that you risk walking into lampposts
in order to keep your ears warm
and cozy. It's knitted in two shades
of a soft bobbly yarn that I've fallen
in love with. And it's chunky—so you
will be able to complete your hat in
just a few evenings.*

Yarn
Bergere de France Toison (77% acrylic,
20% wool, 3% polyamide) chunky yarn
1 x 1¾oz (50g) ball (76yd/70m) in
shade 22641 Blason (A)
1 x 1¾oz (50g) ball (76yd/70m) in
shade 29215 Hennin (B)

Needles and equipment
US 10 (6mm) knitting needles
Yarn sewing needle
4 small safety pins
A pompom maker to make 2¾in (7cm)
pompoms, or two cardboard circles
each measuring 2¾in (7cm) in
diameter with a 1¼in (3cm) diameter
hole in the center.

Gauge (tension)
12 sts and 19 rows in stockinette
(stocking) stitch to a 4-in (10-cm)
square on US 10 (6mm) needles.

Measurements
The finished hat measures approx.
19½in (50cm) circumference and 7in
(18cm) high, excluding earflaps and
pompom.

Abbreviations
See page 126.

For the hat
Cast on 66 sts in A.
Mark the 9th, 20th, 47th, and 58th cast-
on st with a small safety pin (or tie a
piece of contrast-color thread around
the stitch). These mark the places
where you will pick up for the earflaps
once the main hat is finished.
Row 1: [K1, p1] to end.
Rep row 1, 3 times more.
Break A and join in B.
Beg with a k row, work 20 rows in st st.
Row 25: K4, [sk2po, k8] 5 times,
sk2po, k4. *(54 sts)*
Row 26: Purl.
Row 27: K3, [sk2po, k6] 5 times,
sk2po, k3. *(42 sts)*
Row 28: Purl.
Row 29: K2, [sk2po, k4] 5 times,
sk2po, k2. *(30 sts)*
Row 30: Purl.

Row 31: K1, [sk2po, k2] 5 times,
sk2po, k1. *(18 sts)*
Row 32: [P2tog] to end. *(9 sts)*
Break yarn, thread it through rem sts,
and pull up securely.

Earflaps
With the RS facing and using A, pick
up and knit 12 sts between the first
two markers on the cast-on edge (see
page 124).
Knit 7 rows.
Row 8: K1, k2tog, k to last 3 sts, ssk,
k1. *(10 sts)*
Row 9: Knit.
Rep rows 8–9 twice more. *(6 sts)*
Row 14: K1, k2tog, ssk, k1. *(4 sts)*
Row 15: [K2tog] twice. *(2 sts)*
Row 16: K2tog. *(1 st)*
Break yarn and pull it through rem st.
Knit the second earflap in the same
way, between the two remaining
stitch markers.

To make up
Sew the back seam using mattress stitch
(see page 124).
Using the pompom maker or cardboard
circles, make a pompom using A. Trim
the pompom and use the tails of yarn
to sew it to the top of the hat.
Weave in all loose ends.

ZIGZAG BOBBLE HAT

The fashion for all things with chevron stripes is still going strong. So if you fancy trying your hand at two-color knitting that's not too tricky, why not whip yourself up a chevron stripe bobble hat? I've created it in a soft chunky yarn, so it's lovely to wear—and surprisingly quick to knit. Copy me and use this unusual denim blue and pale rust combination—or choose from two of the other lovely shades.

Yarn

Phildar Nebuleuse (41% wool, 41% acrylic, 18% polyamide) chunky yarn
1 x 1¾oz (50g) ball (55yd/51m) in shade 0002 Jeans (A)
1 x 1¾oz (50g) ball (55yd/51m) in shade 0003 Blush (B)

Needles and equipment

US 10 (6mm) knitting needles
US 10½ (6.5mm) knitting needles
Yarn sewing needle
A pompom maker to make 2¾in (7cm) pompoms, or two cardboard circles each measuring 2¾in (7cm) in diameter with a 1¼in (3cm) diameter hole in the center.

Gauge (tension)

12 sts and 17 rows in stockinette (stocking) stitch to a 4-in (10-cm) square on US 10½ (6.5mm) needles.

Measurements

The finished hat measures approx. 20½in (52cm) circumference and 9½in (24cm) high, excluding pompom.

Abbreviations

See page 126.

For the hat

Using US 10 (6mm) needles, cast on 72 sts in A.
Row 1: [K2, p2] to end.
Rep row 1, 5 times more.
Break A and join in B.
Using US 10½ (6.5mm) needles, and beg with a k row, work 2 rows in st st.

Rows 9–15: Work from chart, beg with a k row and using st st.
Break A.
Row 16: Purl.
Rep rows 9–16, twice more.
Row 33: K4, [sl2, k1, p2sso, k7] 6 times, sl2, k1, p2sso, k5. *(58 sts)*
Row 34: [P2tog] to last 2 sts, p2. *(30 sts)*
Row 35: [Sl2, k1, p2sso] to end. *(10 sts)*
Break yarn, thread it through rem sts, and pull up securely.

To make up

Sew the back seam using mattress stitch (see page 124).
Using the pompom maker or cardboard circles, make a pompom in A. Trim the pompom and use the tails of yarn to sew it to the top of the hat. Weave in all loose ends.

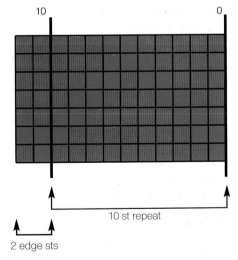

10 st repeat

2 edge sts

key

Jeans (A)

Blush (B)

MULTICOLORED BOBBLE BERET

This traditional beret is perfect for all ages, and will work just as well whether you're dressing up or dressing down. It's knitted entirely in stockinette (stocking) stitch, so is a perfect second or third project for new knitters who are ready to tackle a bit of decreasing. And the multicolored yarn is a godsend, as it means you can create lovely stripes without the hassle of changing yarns. I've added a coordinating pompom to this version—but it would look good plain as well.

Yarn

Lion Brand Unique (100% acrylic) chunky yarn
1 x 3½oz (100g) ball (109yd/100m) in shade 200 Harvest (A)
Debbie Bliss Cashmerino Aran (55% wool, 33% acrylic, 12% cashmere)
1 x 1¾oz (50g) ball (98yd/90m) in shade 502 Lime (B)

Needles and equipment

US 9 (5.5mm) knitting needles
Yarn sewing needle
A pompom maker to make 2¾in (7cm) pompoms, or two cardboard circles each measuring 2¾in (7cm) in diameter with a 1¼in (3cm) diameter hole in the center.

Gauge (tension)

15 sts and 20 rows in stockinette (stocking) stitch to a 4-in (10-cm) square on US 9 (5.5mm) needles.

Measurements

The finished beret measures approx. 18in (46cm) circumference, 11in (28cm) diameter.

For the beret

Cast on 72 sts in A.
Row 1: [K1, p1] to end.
Rep row 1, 5 times more.
Row 7: K3, [m1, k6] 11 times, m1, k3. *(84 sts)*
Beg with a p row, work 17 rows in st st.
Row 25: K6, [k2tog, k12] 5 times, k2tog, k6. *(78 sts)*
Beg with a p row, work 3 rows in st st.
Row 29: K5, [sk2po, k10] 5 times, sk2po, k5. *(66 sts)*
Beg with a p row, work 3 rows in st st.
Row 33: K4, [sk2po, k8] 5 times, sk2po, k4. *(54 sts)*

Beg with a p row, work 3 rows in st st.
Row 37: K3, [sk2po, k6] 5 times, sk2po, k3. *(42 sts)*
Beg with a p row, work 3 rows in st st.
Row 41: K2, [sk2po, k4] 5 times, sk2po, k2. *(30 sts)*
Row 42: Purl.
Row 43: K1, [sk2po, k2] 5 times, sk2po, k1. *(18 sts)*
Row 44: [P2tog] to end. *(9 sts)*
Break yarn, thread it through rem sts, and pull up securely.

To make up

Sew the back seam using mattress stitch (see page 124). Using the pompom maker or cardboard circles, make a pompom in B. Trim the pompom and use the tails of yarn to sew it to the center of the beret. Weave in all loose ends.
The finished beret will need a quick soak and shape (see page 116), to give it its finished shape.

CHUNKY HEADBAND TWO WAYS

It's not quite cold enough for a hat, but it's not quite warm enough to go bare-headed. So what do you do? Knit yourself a range of wooly headbands, of course. These two headbands are knitted in a soft, super-chunky yarn that comes in a whole host of colors—so you can knit a team of headbands to coordinate with every outfit. And you'll easily get two headbands from one ball of yarn—so rifle through your knitting stash and see if you can find any super-chunky yarn oddments just begging for a makeover.

Yarn
Lion Brand Thick & Quick (80% acrylic, 20% wool) super-chunky yarn
1 x 6oz (170g) ball (108yd/98m) in shade 112 Raspberry

Needles and equipment
US 11 (8mm) knitting needles

Gauge (tension)
8 sts and 11 rows in stockinette (stocking) stitch to a 4-in (10-cm) square on US 11 (8mm) needles.

Measurements
The finished ribbed headband measures approx. 16½in (42cm) circumference (unstretched) and 4¼in (11cm) wide.
The finished cable headband measures approx. 20in (50cm) circumference and 4¼in (11cm) wide.

Abbreviations
See page 126.

For the ribbed headband
Cast on 50 sts.
Row 1: [K1, p1] to end.
Rep row 1, 11 times more.
Bind (cast) off pwise.

To make up
Join the two short edges using flat stitch (see page 125).
Weave in all loose ends.

For the cable headband
Cast on 12 sts.
Row 1: Knit.
Row 2: K2, p to last 2 sts, k2.

Row 3: Knit.
Row 4: K2, p to last 2 sts, k2.
Row 5: K2, c8b, k2.
Row 6: K2, p to last 2 sts, k2.
Row 7: Knit.
Row 8: K2, p to last 2 sts, k2.
Rep rows 7–8, twice more.
Rep rows 3–12 (the last 10 rows), 5 times more.
Row 63: Knit.
Row 64: K2, p to last 2 sts, k2.
Row 65: K2, c8b, k2.
Row 66: K2, p to last 2 sts, k2.
Rep rows 7–8 twice.
Bind (cast) off.

To make up
Join the two short edges using flat stitch (see page 125).
Weave in all loose ends.

SIMPLE KNIT BOBBLE HAT

Sometimes, the simple things in life really are the best—and I think this super-chunky, super-quick hat is one them. Knitted mostly in garter stitch and with just some simple decreasing, it's well within the grasp of the newest of new knitters—and an intermediate knitter could probably finish it in just an evening or two. So now you have no excuses. Choose your yarn— I've chosen a lovely soft ice-blue— grab your needles... and go.

Yarn
Lion Brand Wool-Ease Thick & Quick (80% acrylic, 20% wool) super-chunky yarn
1 x 6oz (170g) ball (108yd/98m) in shade 105 Glacier (A)
Sirdar Big Softie (51% wool, 49% acrylic) super-chunky yarn
1 x 1¾oz (50g) ball (49yd/45m) in shade 321 Beanie (B)

Needles and equipment
US 13 (9mm) knitting needles
US 15 (10mm) knitting needles
Yarn sewing needle
A pompom maker to make 4½in (11.5cm) pompoms, or two cardboard circles each measuring 4½in (11.5cm) in diameter with a 2¼in (5.5cm) diameter hole in the center.

Gauge (tension)
9 sts and 12 rows in stockinette (stocking) stitch to a 4-in (10-cm) square on US 15 (10mm) needles.

Measurements
The finished hat measures approx. 20in (50cm) circumference and 10in (25cm) high.

Abbreviations
See page 126.

For the hat
Using US 13 (9mm) needles, cast on 54 sts in A.
Row 1: [K1, p1] to end.
Rep row 1, 3 times more.
Change to US 15 (10mm) needles.
Knit 24 rows.

Row 29: K3, [sk2po, k6] 5 times, sk2po, k3. *(42 sts)*
Row 30: Knit.
Row 31: K2, [sk2po, k4] 5 times, sk2po, k2. *(30 sts)*
Row 32: [K2tog] to end. *(15 sts)*
Row 33: [K2tog] 3 times, k3, [k2tog] 3 times. *(9 sts)*
Break yarn, thread it through rem sts, and pull up securely.

To make up
Sew the back seam using flat stitch (see page 125).
Using the pompom maker or cardboard circles, make a pompom winding A and B together, using A to tie round the pompom center. Trim the pompom and use the tails of yarn to sew it to the top of the hat.
Weave in all loose ends.

TWEEDY TWO-TONE BEANIE

With this two-tone, retro-style bobble hat you'll impress your friends with your knitting skills, as well as your sense of style. The hat is knitted with two shades of yarn—but there's no need to strand the yarns across the back, so it's much easier to make than it looks. I've added a jaunty pompom for a dash of 1970s vibe, but if you want something sleeker, simply leave your hat plain.

Yarn

Debbie Bliss Cashmerino Aran (55% wool, 33% acrylic, 12% cashmere) worsted (Aran) yarn
1 x 1¾oz (50g) ball (98yd/90m) in shade 009 Grey (A)
1 x 1¾oz (50g) ball (98yd/90m) in shade 064 Cowslip (B)

Needles and equipment

US 8 (5mm) knitting needles
Yarn sewing needle
A pompom maker to make 2¾in (7cm) pompoms, or two cardboard circles each measuring 2¾in (7cm) in diameter with a 1¼in (3cm) diameter hole in the center.

Gauge (tension)

18 sts and 24 rows in stockinette (stocking) stitch to a 4-in (10-cm) square on US 8 (5mm) needles.

Measurements

The finished hat measures approx. 17½in (44cm) circumference and 8½in (22cm) high (excluding pompom).

Abbreviations

See page 126.

For the hat

Cast on 81 sts in A.
Knit 6 rows.
Row 7: Using B, [k1, sl1 from left-hand to right-hand needle] to last st, k1.
Row 8: Using B, [k1, yf, sl1 pwise, yb] to last st, k1.
Rows 9–10: Using A, knit.
Row 11: Using B, k1, [k1, sl1 from left-hand to right-hand needle] to last 2 sts, k2.
Row 12: Using B, k2, [yf, sl1pwise, yb, k1] to last st, k1.
Rows 13–14: Using A, knit.
Rep rows 7–14, 5 times more.
Rep rows 7–13 once more.
Row 62: Using A, k3, [k2tog, k6] 4 times, k2tog, k7, [ssk, k6] 4 times, ssk, k3. *(71 sts)*
Rep rows 7–9 once more.

Row 66: Using A, k2, [k2tog, k4] 5 times, k2tog, k3, [ssk, k4] 5 times, ssk, k2. *(59 sts)*
Rep rows 7–9 once more.
Row 70: Using A, k2, [k2tog, k2] 6 times, k2tog, k3, [ssk, k2] 7 times. *(45 sts)*
Rep rows 11–13 once more.
Break B and work remainder of hat in A.
Row 74: [K2tog] 11 times, k1, [ssk] 11 times. *(23 sts)*
Row 75: [K2tog] 5 times, sk2po, [ssk] 5 times. *(11 sts)*
Break yarn, thread it through rem sts, and pull up securely.

To make up

Sew the back seam using flat stitch (see page 125).
Using the pompom maker or cardboard circles, make a pompom in B. Trim the pompom and use the tails of yarn to sew it to the top of the hat.
Weave in all loose ends.

LACY PANELS BEANIE

Soft, delicate, and understated—the perfect hat for so many different occasions. I think that once you've knitted this hat, worn it—and gracefully received all the compliments—you'll want to knit it in a whole range of colors. I've used a gentle shade of lavender—but this hat will look fabulous in whatever shade you pick.

Yarn
Phildar Partner 3.5 (50% polyamide, 25% wool, 25% acrylic) light worsted (DK) yarn
1 x 1¾oz (50g) ball (121yd/111m) in shade 0151 Eglantine

Needles and equipment
US 5 (3.75mm) knitting needles
Yarn sewing needle

Gauge (tension)
23 sts and 30 rows in stockinette (stocking) stitch to a 4-in (10-cm) square on US 5 (3.75mm) needles.

Measurements
The finished hat measures approx. 16in (40cm) circumference and 9½in (24cm) high.

Abbreviations
See page 126.

For the hat
Cast on 98 sts.
Row 1: [K2, p2] to last 2 sts, k2.
Row 2: [P2, k2] to last 2 sts, p2.
Rep rows 1–2, 4 times more.
Row 11: K2, [p1, yo, k2togtbl, p1, k2] to end.
Row 12: P2, [k1, p2] to end.
Row 13: K2, [p1, k2tog, yo, p1, k2] to end.
Row 14: P2, [k1, p2] to end.
Rep rows 11–14, 12 times more.
Row 63: K2tog, [p1, k2tog] to end. *(65 sts)*
Row 64: P1, [k1, p1] to end.
Row 65: K1, [k2tog] to end. *(33 sts)*
Row 66: [P2tog] to last st, p1. *(17 sts)*
Row 67: K1, [k2tog] to end. *(9 sts)*
Break yarn, thread it through rem sts, and pull up securely.

To make up
Sew the back seam using flat stitch (see page 125).
Weave in all loose ends.

FANCY RIB SLOUCHY BEANIE

I love the easy-to-knit but rather impressive-looking fancy rib stitch on this slouchy beanie. So if you're after something super-wearable, but just a tiny bit different, why not give it a go? The alpaca in the wool-mix yarn gives it a luxurious feel, and it's also super-comfy and hard-wearing. The denim shade is great because it goes with practically everything, but as usual, the color is entirely up to you.

Yarn

Katia Peru (40% wool, 40% acrylic, 20% alpaca) chunky yarn
2 x 3½oz (100g) balls (116yd/106m) in shade 18 Light Denim

Needles and equipment

US 10½ (6.5mm) knitting needles

Gauge (tension)

12 sts and 16 rows in stockinette (stocking) stitch to a 4-in (10-cm) square using US 10½ (6.5mm) needles.

Measurements

The finished hat measures approx. 18in (46cm) circumference and 12in (30cm) high.

Abbreviations

See page 126.

For the hat

Cast on 71 sts.
Row 1: [K2, p2] to last 3 sts, k2, p1.
Rep row 1, 47 times more.
Row 49: K1, [sk2po, k1] 17 times, k2tog. *(36 sts)*
Row 50: [K1, p1] to end.
Row 51: K1, [k2tog] to last st, k1. *(19 sts)*
Row 52: P1, [p2tog] to end. *(10 sts)*
Break yarn, thread it through rem sts, and pull up securely.

To make up

Sew the back seam using flat stitch (see page 125).
Weave in all loose ends.

SELF-STRIPED SLOUCHY BEANIE

This side-knitted beanie is one of my favorites, though I'm not sure exactly why. It could be the way the hat shapes itself from the beginning. Or it could be the beautiful simplicity of the stitch. Or perhaps it's the fabulous multicolor yarn that creates a unique pattern as you knit—check out the yarn range to see the amazing selection on offer. I just know that I love it, and I hope you will, too.

Yarn
Cascade 220 Superwash Paints (100% wool) worsted (Aran) yarn
1 x 3½oz (100g) ball (220yd/200m) in shade 9791 Rainbow Sherbert

Needles and equipment
US 6 (4mm) knitting needles
Yarn sewing needle

Gauge (tension)
22 sts and 22 rows in stockinette (stocking) stitch to a 4-in (10-cm) square on US 6 (4mm) needles.

Measurements
The finished hat measures approx. 16in (40cm) circumference and 10½in (27cm) high.

Abbreviations
See page 126.

For the hat
Cast on 48 sts.
Row 1: Knit.
Row 2: K47, WT.
Row 3: Knit.
Row 4: K45, WT.
Row 5: Knit.
Row 6: K43, WT.
Row 7: Knit.
Row 8: K41, WT.
Row 9: Knit.
Row 10: K39, WT.
Row 11: Knit.
Row 12: K37, WT.
Row 13: Knit.
Row 14: K35, WT.
Row 15: Knit.
Row 16: K33, WT.
Row 17: Knit.
Row 18: K31, WT.
Row 19: Knit.

Rows 20–21: Knit 2 rows.
Rep rows 1–21, 5 times more.
Cast (bind) off.
Rep rows 1–19 once more.
Bind (cast) off.

To make up
Sew the back seam using flat stitch (see page 125).
Weave in all loose ends.

LACY CLOCHE WITH FLOWER

There's no reason why you can't keep the mood soft and romantic while also keeping yourself cozy. This snug-fitting hat, knitted in an oh-so-simple lace stitch in a beautiful light mohair-mix yarn, will make sure you don't have to sacrifice style for practicality when you're out for a brisk stroll. And if you want that extra dash of je ne sais quoi, *don't forget the flower.*

Yarn
Rowan Kid Classic (70% lambswool, 22% kid mohair, 8% polyamide) worsted (Aran) yarn
1 x 1¾oz (50g) ball (153yd/140m) in shade 828 Feather (A)
1 x 1¾oz (50g) ball (153yd/140m) in shade 882 Lime (B)
1 x 1¾oz (50g) ball (153yd/140m) in shade 883 Water (C)

Needles and equipment
US 8 (5mm) knitting needles
Yarn sewing needle
Standard sewing needle

Other materials
1 x ⅜-in (1cm) white pearl bead
Cream sewing thread

Gauge (tension)
20 sts and 25 rows in stockinette (stocking) stitch to a 4-in (10-cm) square on US 8 (5mm) needles.

Measurements
The finished hat measures approx. 19½in (48cm) circumference and 7in (18cm) high.

Abbreviations
See page 126.

For the hat
Note that the first row will be the WS.
Cast on 84 sts in A.
Purl 5 rows.
Row 6 (RS): [Yo, skpo] to end.
Purl 2 rows.
Break A and join in B.
Row 9: Purl.
Row 10: [Yo, skpo] to end.
Purl 2 rows.
Rep rows 9–12 (last 4 rows), 3 times more.
Break B and join in C.
Row 25: Purl.
Row 26: [Yo, skpo] to end.
Purl 2 rows.
Rep rows 25–28 (last 4 rows) once more.
Row 33: P2, [p2tog, p4] to last 4 sts, p2tog, p2. *(70 sts)*
Row 34: [Yo, skpo] to end.
Row 35: Purl.
Row 36: P4, [p2tog, p4] to end. *(59 sts)*
Row 37: P2, [p2tog, p2] 7 times, p1, [p2tog, p2] 7 times. *(45 sts)*
Row 38: [Yo, skpo] 11 times, k1, [yo, skpo] to end.
Row 39: Purl.

Row 40: P2, [p2tog, p2] 5 times, p3, [p2tog, p2] to end. *(35 sts)*
Row 41: [P2tog] 8 times, p3, [p2tog] to end. *(19 sts)*
Row 42: [P2tog] 4 times, p3, [p2tog] to end. *(11 sts)*
Break yarn, thread it through rem sts, and pull up securely.

For the flower
Cast on 10 sts in A.
Row 1: [Inc] twice. *(4 sts)*
Turn, and work on 4 sts just knitted only.
Beg with a p row, work 11 rows in st st.
Next row: K2tog, ssk, lift right-hand st over left-hand st. *(1 st)*
Next row: K1 into next cast-on st, inc. Turn and work on 4 sts just worked only.
Beg with a p row, work 11 rows in st st.
Next row: K2tog, ssk, lift right-hand st over left-hand st. ** *(1 st)*
Rep from * to ** 3 times more.
Knit 1 into first cast-on st to complete the final petal. *(2 sts)*
Bind (cast) off 1 st, break yarn, and pull it through rem st.

To make up
Sew the back seam using flat stitch (see page 125).
Stitch the flower in place. Using cream sewing thread, sew on the bead in the center of the flower.
Weave in all loose ends.

FLOWER-PIN BEANIE

In springtime, Mother Nature's flowers push their way out of the ground, so why shouldn't you show off your springtime colors and create your own flower, too? This pattern, with its slightly fancy edging, is aimed at the more confident knitter. But if you've already knitted up a few of the simpler hats in this collection, surely it's time to give this one a go?

Yarn
Rowan All Seasons Cotton (60% cotton, 40% acrylic) worsted (Aran) yarn
1 x 1¾oz (50g) ball (98yd/90m) in shade 246 Hedge (A)
1 x 1¾oz (50g) ball (98yd/90m) in shade 257 Dark Violet (B)
1 x 1¾oz (50g) ball (98yd/90m) in shade 255 Summer (C)

Needles and equipment
US 9 (5.5mm) knitting needles
Yarn sewing needle
Standard sewing needle

Other materials
1 x ¾-in (18-mm) pink button
Pale pink sewing thread

Gauge (tension)
18 sts and 25 rows in stockinette (stocking) stitch to a 4-in (10-cm) square on US 9 (5.5mm) needles.

Measurements
The finished hat measures approx. 19in (48cm) circumference and 7½in (19cm) high.

Abbreviations
See page 126.

For the hat border
Using A, cast on 3 sts.
Cast (bind) off 2 sts. *(1 st)*
Transfer st from right-hand to left-hand needle.
*Knit into front, back, then front again of st. *(3 sts)*
Cast (bind) off 2 sts. *(1 st)*
Transfer st from right-hand to left-hand needle.**
Rep from * to ** 39 times more.
Next row: Knit into front, back, then front again of st.
Cast (bind) off 2 sts. *(1 st)*

For the hat
Do not turn but work across straight edge of border. *(1 st on right-hand needle)*

Row 1: [Yo, k1 into loop of picot shape] to end. *(83 sts)*
Row 2: Knit.
Break A and join in B.
Row 3: Knit.
Row 4: K1, [p1, k3] to last 2 sts, p1, k1.
Row 5: K3, [p1, k3] to end.
Row 6: K1, [p1, k3] to last 2 sts, p1, k1.
Rep rows 5–6, 18 times more.
Row 43: K2, [p3tog, k1] to last st, k1. *(43 sts)*
Row 44: [K1, p1] to last st, k1.
Row 45: [K2tog] to last st, k1. *(22 sts)*
Row 46: [P2tog] to end. *(11 sts)*
Break yarn, thread through rem sts, and pull up securely.

Flower
Cast on 8 sts in C.
*Row 1: Inc, k to end. *(9 sts)*
Knit 2 rows.
Row 4: K6, k2tog, k1. *(8 sts)*
Cast (bind) off 7 sts pwise. *(1 st)***
Cast on 7 sts. *(8 sts)*
Rep from * to ** 4 times more.
Break yarn and pull it through rem st.
Gather along straight edge, pull up tightly, and secure.

To make up
Sew the back seam using flat stitch (see page 125).
Sew the flower in place and sew on the button in the center of the flower.
Weave in all loose ends.

TEXTURED BEANIE

This close-fitting, traditional beanie is knitted in a lovely, slightly knobbly stitch. But don't worry, it's very easy to get the hang of once you've worked a few rows, so it's suitable for advanced beginners, as well as more experienced knitters. The yarn has a hint of cashmere, so it's wonderfully soft, and it comes in a range of shades that are so beautiful, you may find it hard to stop at knitting just one of these hats.

Yarn

Debbie Bliss Cashmerino Aran
(50% wool, 33% acrylic, 12%
cashmere) worsted (Aran) yarn
1 x 1¾oz (50g) ball (98yd/90m) in
shade 010 Teal (A)
2 x 1¾oz (50g) balls (98yd/90m) in
shade 061 Jade (B)

Needles and equipment

US 8 (5mm) knitting needles
Yarn sewing needle

Gauge (tension)

18 sts and 24 rows in stockinette
(stocking) stitch to a 4-in (10-cm)
square using US 8 (5mm) needles.

Measurements

The finished hat measures approx.
17in (44cm) circumference and 8in
(20cm) high.

For the hat

Cast on 91 sts in A.
Row 1: [K1, p1] to last st, k1.
Row 2: [P1, k1] to last st, p1.
Rep rows 1–2 twice more.
Break A and join in B.
Row 7: Knit.
Row 8: Purl.
Row 9: [K1, sl1] to last st, k1.
Row 10: [K1, yf, sl1, yb] to last st, k1.
Rep rows 7–10, 10 times more.
Row 51: Knit.
Row 52: P5, [sl1 kwise, p2tog, psso, p13] twice, sl1 kwise, p2tog, psso, p11, [sl1 kwise, p2tog, psso, p13] twice, sl1 kwise, p2tog, psso, p5. *(79 sts)*
Row 53: [K1, sl1] to last st, k1.
Row 54: [K1, yf, sl1, yb] to last st, k1.
Row 55: Knit.
Row 56: P3, [sl1 kwise, p2tog, psso, p11] 5 times, sl1 kwise, p2tog, psso, p3. *(67 sts)*
Row 57: [K1, sl1] to last st, k1.
Row 58: [K1, yf, sl1, yb] to last st, k1.
Row 59: Knit.

Row 60: P1, [sl1 kwise, p2tog, psso, p1] 8 times, p2, [sl1 kwise, p2tog, psso, p1] 8 times. *(35 sts)*
Row 61: [K2tog] 8 times, k3, [k2tog] 8 times. *(19 sts)*
Row 62: [P2tog] 4 times, p3, [p2tog] 4 times. *(11 sts)*
Break yarn, thread it through rem sts, and pull up securely.

To make up

Sew the back seam using flat stitch
(see page 125) and matching yarns.
Weave in all loose ends.

RETRO BOBBLE HAT

I'm always on the lookout for two-color projects that don't involve stranding the yarn across the back of your work—which can be a wee bit tricky for newbie knitters. So this knitting stitch, which has a bit of a pineapple look about it—matches my requirements perfectly. It looks time-consuming and tricky, but once you've got into the swing, it's satisfyingly simple. I love its retro feel and added a bobble to mine—but, as usual, the choice is yours.

Yarn
Sublime Baby Cashmere Merino Silk DK (75% wool, 20% silk, 5% cashmere) light worsted (DK) yarn
1 x 1¾oz (50g) ball (127yd/116m) in shade 337 Elkin (A)
1 x 1¾oz (50g) ball (127yd/116m) in shade 195 Puzzle (B)

Needles and equipment
US 6 (4mm) knitting needles
Yarn sewing needle
A pompom maker to make 2¾in (7cm) pompoms, or two cardboard circles each measuring 2¾in (7cm) in diameter with a 1¼in (3cm) diameter hole in the center.

Gauge (tension)
22 sts and 28 rows in stockinette (stocking) stitch to a 4-in (10-cm) square on US 6 (4mm) needles.

Measurements
The finished hat measures approx. 16in (40cm) circumference and 9½in (24cm) high.

Abbreviations
See page 126.
Note that all stitches are slipped purlwise.

For the hat
Cast on 104 sts in A.
Row 1: [K1, p1] to end.
Rep row 1, 10 times more.
Row 12: Knit.
Leave A at side and join in B.
Row 13: In B, k1, sl1, [k4, sl2] to last 6 sts, k4, sl1, k1.
Row 14: In B, p1, sl1, [p4, sl2] to last 6 sts, p4, sl1, p1.
Leave B at side.
Row 15: In A, k1, sl1, [k4, sl2] to last 6 sts, k4, sl1, k1.
Row 16: In A, k1, yf, sl1, yb, [k4, yf, sl2, yb) to last 6 sts, k4, yf, sl1, yb, k1.
Leave A at side.
Row 17: In B, k3, [sl2, k4] to last 5 sts, sl2, k3.

Row 18: In B, p3, [sl2, p4] to last 5 sts, sl2, p3.
Leave B at side.
Row 19: In A, k3, [sl2, k4] to last 5 sts, sl2, k3.
Row 20: In A, k3, [yf, sl2, yb, k4] to last 5 sts, yf, sl2, yb, k3.
Rep rows 13–20, 7 times more.
Cont in A only.
Row 77: [K2tog, k4] to last 2 sts, k2tog. *(86 sts)*
Row 78: P2, p2tog, [p3, p2tog] to last 2 sts, p2. *(69 sts)*
Row 79: K1, [sk2po, k1] to end. *(35 sts)*
Row 80: P1, [p2tog] 8 times, p1, [p2tog] 8 times, p1. *(19 sts)*
Row 81: K1, [k2tog] 4 times, k1, [k2tog] 4 times, k1. *(11 sts)*
Break yarn, thread it through rem sts, and pull up securely.

To make up
Sew the back seam using mattress stitch (see page 124).
Using the pompom maker or cardboard circles, make a pompom, using B. Trim the pompom and use the tails of yarn to sew it to the top of the hat.
Weave in all loose ends.

CABLE-BAND BERET

If you want something classic, but not too classic, then this could be the beret for you. Knitted in a wool-rich yarn, I've added a twist to the standard beret by knitting a twisty cable along the band. I chose a zingy pink for this beret—but the yarn comes in all sorts of gorgeous shades so the choice, as always, is up to you. And because the yarn is chunky, you'll find your beret will come together much more quickly than you think.

Yarn
Katia Maxi Merino (55% wool, 45% acrylic) chunky yarn
1 x 3½oz (100g) ball (137yd/125m) in shade 42

Needles and equipment
US 8 (5mm) knitting needles
US 9 (5.5mm) knitting needles
Yarn sewing needle
Medium/large cable needle

Gauge (tension)
13 stitches and 18 rows in stockinette (stocking) stitch to a 4-in (10-cm) square on US 9 (5.5mm) needles.

Measurements
The finished beret measures approx. 20in (50cm) circumference and 10½in (27cm) diameter.

Abbreviations
See page 126.

For the beret band
Using US 8 (5mm) needles, cast on 13 sts.
Row 1: P2, k9, p2.
Row 2: K2, p9, k2.
Row 3: P2, k9, p2.
Row 4: K2, p9, k2.
Row 5: P2, k9, p2.
Row 6: K2, p9, k2.
Row 7: P2, k3, c6f, p2.
Row 8: K2, p9, k2.
Row 9: P2, k9, p2.
Row 10: K2, p9, k2.
Row 11: P2, k9, p2.
Row 12: K2, p9, k2.
Row 13: P2, c6b, k3, p2.
Row 14: K2, p9, k2.
Row 15: P2, k9, p2.
Row 16: K2, p9, k2.
Row 17: P2, k9, p2.
Row 18: K2, p9, k2.
Rep rows 7–18, 6 times more, then rows 7–10 again.

For the beret
With RS of band facing and beg at cast-on edge, and using US 9 (5.5mm) needles, pick up and knit 90 sts evenly across one long side of the cable band.
Beg with a p row, work 13 rows in st st.
Next row: K6, [sk2po, k12] 5 times, sk2po, k6. *(78 sts)*
Beg with a p row, work 3 rows in st st.
Next row: K5, [sk2po, k10] 5 times, sk2po, k5. *(66 sts)*
Beg with a p row, work 3 rows in st st.
Next row: K4, [sk2po, k8] 5 times, sk2po, k4. *(54 sts)*
Beg with a p row, work 3 rows in st st.
Next row: K3, [sk2po, k6] 5 times, sk2po, k3. *(42 sts)*
Next row: Purl.
Next row: K2, [sk2po, k4] 5 times, sk2po, k2. *(30 sts)*
Next row: Purl.
Next row: K1, [sk2po, k2] 5 times, sk2po, k1. *(18 sts)*
Next row: [P2tog] to end. *(9 sts)*
Next row: [K2tog] twice, k1, [ssk] twice. *(5 sts)*
Next row: Purl.
Next row: Knit.
Cast (bind) off pwise.

To make up
Sew the back seam of the beret, including the spike at the top, using mattress stitch (see page 124).
Weave in all loose ends.
The finished beret will need a quick soak and shape (see page 116), to give it its finished shape.

SIMPLE SIDEWAYS BEANIE

This head-hugging beanie is worked in garter stitch only—the simplest of all stitches. It's knitted in a chunky yarn, but it's a cotton mix so the hat is ideal for those slightly chilly early spring and late summer days. Rather unusually, the beanie is knitted sideways; the crown is shaped by knitting slightly shorter rows. But don't worry about this—it's a very clever technique that's super-easy to learn.

Yarn
Rowan All Seasons Chunky (60% cotton, 40% acrylic) chunky yarn
1 x 3½oz (100g) ball (93yd/85m) in shade 607 Cove

Needles and equipment
US 10½ (7mm) knitting needles
Yarn sewing needle

Gauge (tension)
11 sts and 16 rows in stockinette (stocking) stitch to a 4-in (10-cm) square on US 10½ (7mm) needles.

Measurements
The finished hat measures approx. 20½in (52cm) circumference and 8¼in (21cm) high.

Abbreviations
See page 126.

For the hat
Cast on 24 sts.
Row 1: Knit.
Row 2: K23, WT.
Row 3: Knit.
Row 4: K21, WT.
Row 5: Knit.
Row 6: K19, WT.
Row 7: Knit.
Row 8: K17, WT.
Row 9: Knit.
Row 10: K15, WT.
Row 11: Knit.
Row 12: K13, WT.
Row 13: Knit.

Row 14: Knit.
Rep rows 1–14, 5 times more.
Rep rows 1–13 once more.
Bind (cast) off.

To make up
Sew the back seam using flat stitch (see page 125).
Weave in all loose ends.

CABLE BERET

Who can resist the sophistication of a beret, a soft yarn, and a classic cable? I've chosen a soft shade of fawn for this beret, but the lovely Italian-spun yarn comes in a great range of neutrals and classics with something to suit everyone and complement almost every outfit. The cable is very simple to work and this beret would be a great first project if you're just standing on the edge, ready to dive into the world of cable knitting.

Yarn
Rico Design Fashion Highland Chunky (70% acrylic, 30% wool) chunky yarn 1 x 1¾oz (50g) ball (109yd/100m) in shade 001 Beige

Needles and equipment
US 10 (6mm) knitting needles
Medium-large cable needle

Gauge (tension)
14 sts and 19 rows in stockinette (stocking) stitch to a 4-in (10-cm) square on US 10 (6mm) needles.

Measurements
The finished beret measures approx. 18in (46cm) circumference, 10½in (27cm) diameter.

Abbreviations
See page 126.

For the beret
Cast on 66 sts.
Row 1: [K1, p1] to end.
Rep row 1, 5 times more.
Row 7: K1, m1, [k3, m1] 10 times, k1, m1, k2, m1, k1, [m1, k3] 10 times, m1, k1. *(90 sts)*
Row 8: K2, [p6, k4] 8 times, p6, k2.
Row 9: P2, [k6, p4] 8 times, k6, p2.
Row 10: K2, [p6, k4] 8 times, p6, k2.
Row 11: P2, [k6, p4] 8 times, k6, p2.
Row 12: K2, [p6, k4] 8 times, p6, k2.
Row 13: P2, [c6b, p4] 8 times, c6b, p2.
Row 14: K2, [p6, k4] 8 times, p6, k2.
Rep rows 9–14, twice more.
Row 27: P2, [k6, p4] 8 times, k6, p2.
Row 28: K2, [p6, k4] 8 times, p6, k2.

Row 29: P2, [k6, p2tog, p2tog] 8 times, k6, p2. *(74 sts)*
Row 30: K2, [p6, k2] 9 times.
Row 31: P2, [c6b, p2] 9 times.
Row 32: K2, [p6, k2] 9 times.
Row 33: P2, [k6, p2] 9 times.
Row 34: K2, [p6, k2] 9 times.
Row 35: P2tog, [k6, p2tog] 9 times. *(64 sts)*
Row 36: K1, [p6, k1] 9 times.
Row 37: P1, [c6b, p1] 9 times.
Row 38: K1, [p6, k1] 9 times.
Row 39: P1, [k6, p1] 9 times.
Row 40: K1, [p6, k1] 9 times.
Row 41: P1, [ssk, k2, k2tog, p1] 9 times. *(46 sts)*
Row 42: K1, [p4, k1] 9 times.
Row 43: P1, [c4b, p1] 9 times.
Row 44: K1, [p4, k1] 9 times.
Row 45: P1, [k4, p1] 9 times.
Row 46: K1, [p4, k1] 9 times.
Row 47: P1, [ssk, k2tog, p1] 9 times. *(28 sts)*
Row 48: K1, [p2tog, k1] to end. *(19 sts)*
Row 49: [Skpo] to last st, k1. *(10 sts)*
Break yarn, thread it through rem sts, and pull up securely.

To make up
Sew the side seam of the beret using mattress stitch (see page 124). Weave in all loose ends.
The finished beret will need a quick soak and shape (see page 116), to give it its finished shape.

SLOUCHY BEANIE WITH BUTTONS

Bang up to date, this comfortable, slouchy beanie is knitted from a beautiful wool and alpaca-blend yarn. I've knitted this one in a gentle turquoise—but the yarn is available in a range of lovely shades, suitable for the boys and gents in your life as well as the girls and ladies. The lovely texture is a simple combination of knit and purl stitches, so it is an ideal project for those wanting to branch out from garter and stockinette (stocking) stitch—but not yet ready for the lacy look. Best of all, this generously sized hat takes just one ball of yarn.

Yarn
Rowan Creative Focus Worsted (75% wool, 25% alpaca) worsted (Aran) yarn 1 x 3½oz (100g) ball (220yd/200m) in shade 00007 Lapis

Needles and equipment
US 8 (5mm) knitting needles
Yarn sewing needle

Other materials
Two ⅞-in (21-mm) pink buttons

Gauge (tension)
18 sts and 22 rows in stockinette (stocking) stitch to a 4-in (10-cm) square on US 8 (5mm) needles.

Measurements
The finished hat measures approx. 18in (46cm) circumference and 10½in (27cm) high.

Abbreviations
See page 126.

For the hat
Cast on 91 sts.
Row 1: [K1, p1] to last st, k1.
Row 2: [P1, k1] to last st, p1.
Rep rows 1–2, 8 times more.
Row 19: [K1, p1] to last st, k1.
Row 20 (WS): [K1, p2] to last st, k1.
Row 21: [P1, k2] to last st, p1.
Row 22: Knit.
Row 23: Purl.
Rep rows 20–23, 13 times more.
Row 76: [K1, p2] to last st, k1.
Row 77: [P1, k2] to last st, p1.
Row 78: [K1, k2tog] to last st, k1.
(61 sts)
Row 79: Purl.
Row 80: [P1, k1] to last st, p1.

Row 81: K1, [k2tog] to last 2 sts, k2. *(32 sts)*
Row 82: P1, [p2tog] to last st, p1. *(17 sts)*
Bind (cast) off.

To make up
Fold the rim of the hat up on the RS, so that the cast-on edge of the ribbing meets the part where the ribbing ends and the textured knitting begins. Slip stitch the cast-on edge of the ribbing in place.
Sew the back seam using flat stitch (see page 125).
Weave in all loose ends.
Using an unraveled strand of knitting yarn, sew the buttons in place on the side of the hat.

DIAGONALS BERET

When you need a hat that creates a bit of style as well as keeping you warm, a lacy beret, knitted in a super-soft, super-fluffy yarn is a great solution. I've knitted this one in a stunning deep turquoise—but the yarn comes in lots of other equally lovely jewel shades, so take a look and see which one you fall in love with. Like most types of lacy knitting, this is easier than it looks—in fact, I think it's one of the most simple lace knits out and suitable even if you're brand new to lacy knitting.

Yarn
Phildar Beaugency (55% polyamide, 25% acrylic, 20% wool) worsted (Aran) yarn
1 x 1¾oz (50g) ball (89yd/82m) in shade 0024 Persan

Needles and equipment
US 8 (5mm) knitting needles
US 10½ (6.5mm) knitting needles
Yarn sewing needle

Gauge (tension)
14 sts and 17 rows in stockinette (stocking) stitch to a 4-in (10-cm) square on US 10½ (6.5mm) needles.

Measurements
The finished beret measures approx. 22in (56cm) circumference and 11¼in (29cm) diameter.

Abbreviations
See page 126.

For the beret
Using US 8 (5mm) needles, cast on 77 sts.
Row 1: [K1, p1] to last st, k1.
Row 2: [P1, k1] to last st, p1.
Rep rows 1–2 once more, then row 1 again.
Change to US 10½ (6.5mm) needles.
Row 7: K2, [yo, ssk, k1] to end.
Row 8: Purl.
Row 9: K3, [yo, ssk, k1] to last 2 sts, k2.
Row 10: Purl.
Row 11: K1, [yo, ssk, k1] to last st, k1.
Row 12: Purl.
Rep rows 7–12, 4 times more.
Row 37: K1, [k2tog, k1] to last st, k1.
(52 sts)
Row 38: Purl.
Row 39: K1, [k2tog] to last st, k1.
(27 sts)
Row 40: P1, [p2tog] to end. *(14 sts)*
Break yarn, thread it through rem sts, and pull up securely.

Making up and finishing
Sew the back seam of the beret using flat stitch (see page 125).
Weave in all loose ends.

CABLED SLOUCHY BEANIE

In the world of beanie hats, this is an absolute classic that everyone loves. It's chunky and it's got lots of cables. If you're new to cables, this is an ideal first project. Ask any experienced knitter about cables, and they'll all tell you the same story: They're much, much easier to work than you might imagine. So grab a cable needle, try out a few cables... then get to work on this hat.

Yarn

Bergère de France Magic + (50% wool, 50% acrylic) chunky yarn
2 x 1¾oz (50g) balls (87yd/80m) in shade 25466 Sepale

Needles and equipment

US 9 (5.5mm) knitting needles
Medium-size cable needle
Yarn sewing needle

Gauge (tension)

16 sts and 22 rows in stockinette (stocking) stitch to a 4-in (10-cm) square on US 9 (5.5mm) needles.

Measurements

The finished hat measures approx. 17in (44cm) circumference and 10½in (27cm) high.

Abbreviations

See page 126.

For the hat

Cast on 88 sts.
Row 1: [K1, p1] to end.
Rep row 1, 5 times more.
Row 7: P2, [k4, p1] to last st, p1.
Row 8: K2, [p4, k1] to last st, k1.
Rep rows 7–8 once more.
Row 11: P2, [c4b, p1, k4, p1] to last 6 sts, c4b, p2.
Row 12: K2, [p4, k1] to last st, k1.
Row 13: P2, [k4, p1] to last st, p1.
Row 14: K2, [p4, k1] to last st, k1.
Rep rows 13–14 once more.
Row 17: P2, [k4, p1, c4b, p1] to last 6 sts, k4, p2.
Row 18: K2, [p4, k1] to last st, k1.
Row 19: P2, [k4, p1] to last st, p1.
Row 20: K2, [p4, k1] to last st, k1.
Rep rows 19–20 once more.
Rep rows 11–22 (last 12 rows) twice more.
Rep rows 11–14 once more.
Row 51: P2, [k1, k2tog, k1, p1] to last st, p1. *(71 sts)*
Row 52: K2, [p3, k1] to last st, k1.
Row 53: P2, [sk2po, p1] to last st, p1. *(37 sts)*

Row 54: K2, [p1, k1] to last st, k1.
Row 55: P2tog, [sl1, p1, psso] to last st, p1. *(19 sts)*
Row 56: [P2tog] to last st, p1. *(10 sts)*
Break yarn, thread it through rem sts, and pull up securely.

To make up

Sew the back seam using flat stitch (see page 125).
Weave in all loose ends.

BUTTON-TRIM BERET

With a touch of the 1960s but also bang up to date, this beret should thrill any modern vintage fan. It's knitted in a soft wool-mix yarn and worked on big needles—so you'll find it comes together pretty quickly. I've knitted this version in a gorgeous sugar-almond pink, which I thought would be perfect for breezy days in spring. But the yarn range includes all types of colors, so have a browse through and grab your favorite.

Yarn
Lion Brand Wool-Ease Thick & Quick (80% acrylic, 20% wool) super-chunky yarn
1 x 6oz (170g) ball (106yd/97m) in shade 103 Blossom

Needles and equipment
US 13 (9mm) knitting needles
US 15 (10mm) knitting needles
Yarn sewing needle
Standard sewing needle

Other materials
1 x 1in (25mm) deep pink button
Pale pink sewing thread

Gauge (tension)
8 sts and 11 rows in stockinette (stocking) stitch to a 4-in (10-cm) square on US 15 (10mm) needles.

Measurements
The finished beret measures approx. 19½in (50cm) circumference and 11½in (29cm) in diameter.

Abbreviations
See page 126.

For the beret band
Using US 13 (9mm) needles, cast on 5 sts.
Row 1: Sl1, k to end.
Row 2: Purl.
Rep rows 1–2, 32 times more.
Cast (bind) off 4 sts, leaving 1 st rem on needle.

For the beret
With RS facing and using US 15 (10mm) needles, beg at cast-on edge, pick up and knit 60 sts along the top edge of the band, working one stitch into the stitch at the end of every row. (You will have a short length [6 rows] of the band left which will overlap the button on the finished beret.)

Beg with a p row, work 13 rows in st st.
Row 14: K4, [k2tog, k8] 5 times, k2tog, k4. *(54 sts)*
Beg with a p row, work 3 rows in st st.
Row 18: K3, [sk2po, k6] 5 times, sk2po, k3. *(42 sts)*
Beg with a p row, work 3 rows in st st.
Row 22: K2, [sk2po, k4] 5 times, sk2po, k2. *(30 sts)*
Row 23: Purl.
Row 24: K1, [sk2po, k2] 5 times, sk2po, k1. *(18 sts)*
Row 25: [P2tog] to end. *(9 sts)*
Break yarn, thread it through rem sts, and pull up securely.

To make up
Sew the seam of the main part of the beret only using mattress stitch (see page 124).
Sew the button in place and overlap the loose end of the beret band, using a gap in the knitting as a buttonhole.
Weave in all loose ends.
The finished beret will need a quick soak and shape (see page 116), to give it its finished shape.

CABLE RIB BEANIE

Classic this beanie might be, but there's a contemporary twist in the cable-look rib, which you can work without the bother of a cable needle. I've knitted this version in a deep shade of gold and added a contrasting pompom in two shades of gray. You can, of course, knit your own version in whatever color you fancy—and the pompoms are a great way of using up all those oddments of yarns. You can make your pompom in two shades like this one—or one shade, or three... or just whatever you fancy.

Yarn
Lion Brand Wool-Ease (80% acrylic, 20% wool) worsted (Aran) yarn
1 x 3oz (85g) ball (197yd/180m) in shade 171 Gold (A)
Sirdar Country Style DK (40% nylon, 30% wool, 30% acrylic) light worsted (DK) yarn
1 x 1¾oz (50g) ball (170yd/155m) in shade 395 Anthracite (B)
1 x 1¾oz (50g) ball (170yd/155m) in shade 434 Silver Cloud (C)

Needles and equipment
US 7 (4.5mm) knitting needles
Yarn sewing needle
A pompom maker to make 3½-in (9cm) pompoms or two cardboard circles each measuring 3½in (9cm) in diameter with a 1½in (4cm) diameter hole in the center.

Gauge (tension)
20 sts and 22 rows in stockinette (stocking) stitch to a 4-in (10-cm) square on US 7 (4.5mm) needles.

Measurements
The finished hat measures approx. 16in (40cm) circumference (unstretched) and 9in (23cm) high, excluding pompom.

Abbreviations
See page 126.

For the hat
Cast on 102 sts in A.
Row 1: P2, [k2, p2] to end.
Row 2: K2, [p2, k2] to end.
Row 3: P2, [RT, p2] to end.
Row 4: K2, [p2, k2] to end.
Rep rows 1–4, 3 times more.
Beg with a k row, work 24 rows in st st.
Row 41: K7, [sl2, k1, p2sso, k14] 5 times, sl2, k1, p2sso, k7. *(90 sts)*

Row 42: Purl.
Row 43: K6, [sl2, k1, p2sso, k12] 5 times, sl2, k1, p2sso, k6. *(78 sts)*
Row 44: Purl.
Row 45: K5, [sl2, k1, p2sso, k10] 5 times, sl2, k1, p2sso, k5. *(66 sts)*
Row 46: Purl.
Row 47: K4, [sl2, k1, p2sso, k8] 5 times, sl2, k1, p2sso, k4. *(54 sts)*
Row 48: Purl.
Row 49: K3, [sl2, k1, p2sso, k6] 5 times, sl2, k1, p2sso, k3. *(42 sts)*
Row 50: Purl.
Row 51: K2, [sl2, k1, p2sso, k4] 5 times, sl2, k1, p2sso, k2. *(30 sts)*
Row 52: Purl.
Row 53: K1, [sl2, k1, p2sso, k2] 5 times, sl2, k1, p2sso, k1. *(18 sts)*
Row 54: [P2tog] to end. *(9 sts)*
Break yarn, thread it through rem sts, and pull up securely.

To make up
Sew the back seam using flat stitch (see page 125).
Using the pompom maker or cardboard circles, make a pompom, winding yarns B and C together. Trim the pompom and use the tail of yarn to attach it to the top of the hat.
Weave in all loose ends.

PEAKED NEWSBOY BERET

The newsboy cap, newsy cap, baker boy... call it what you like. This peaked hat from bygone days has had something of a resurgence of late—and now you can knit your very own super-slouchy version to add a dash of casual class to your winter outfits. The stitch is quite heavily textured, but is nothing more than a double seed (moss) stitch, which is oh-so-simple to do. I've knitted this hat in a pure wool yarn in the palest of grays, which I thought would go well with loads of different colored outfits. But as usual, the choice is completely down to you.

Yarn

Debbie Bliss Rialto Chunky (100% wool) chunky yarn
3 x 1¾oz (50g) balls (66yd/60m) in shade 02 Silver

Needles and equipment

US 9 (5.5mm) knitting needles
US 10½ (6.5mm) knitting needles
Yarn sewing needle

Other materials

An 8¼ x 4in (21 x 10cm) piece of thick clear plastic or similar material for stiffening the peak

Gauge (tension)

15 sts and 21 rows in stockinette (stocking) stitch to a 4-in (10-cm) square on US 10½ (6.5mm) needles.

Measurements

The hat measures approx. 18in (46cm) circumference and 8¼in (21cm) high.

Abbreviations

See page 126.

For the hat

Using US 9 (5.5mm) needles, cast on 66 sts, placing a marker after 21st st and 45th st.
Row 1: [K2, p2] to last 2 sts, k2.
Row 2: [P2, k2] to last 2 sts, p2.
Rep rows 1–2 once more.
Row 5: [K3, m1] to last 3 sts, k3. *(87 sts)*
Change to US 10½ (6.5mm) needles and use these to knit the rest of the hat, including the peak.
Row 6 (RS): [K1, p1] to last st, k1.
Row 7: [P1, k1] to last st, p1.
Row 8: [P1, k1] to last st, p1.
Row 9: [K1, p1] to last st, k1.
Rep rows 6–9, 5 times more.
Row 30: [K1, p1] to last st, k1.
Row 31: [P1, k1] 3 times, sl2 pwise, p1, psso, ([k1, p1] 4 times, k1, sl2 pwise, p1, psso) 6 times, [k1, p1] 3 times. *(73 sts)*
Row 32: [P1, k1] to last st, p1.
Row 34: [K1, p1] twice, k1, sl2 pwise, p1, psso, ([k1, p1] 3 times, k1, sl2 pwise, p1, psso) 6 times, [k1, p1] twice, k1. *(59 sts)*
Row 35: [K1, p1] to last st, k1.
Row 36: [P1, k1] twice, sl2 pwise, p1, psso, ([k1, p1] twice, k1, sl2 pwise, p1, psso) 6 times, [p1, k1] twice. *(45 sts)*
Row 37: [P1, k1] to end.
Row 38: K1, p1, k1, sl2 pwise, p1, psso, [k1, p1, k1, sl2pwise, p1, psso] 6 times, k1, p1, k1. *(31 sts)*
Row 39: [K1, p1] to last st, k1.
Row 40: P1, k1, [sl2 pwise, p1, psso, k1] 7 times, p1. *(17 sts)*
Row 41: [P1, k1] to last st, p1.
Row 42: K1, [sl2 pwise, p1, psso] 5 times, k1. *(7 sts)*
Break yarn, thread it through rem sts, and pull up securely.

For the peak

Using US 10½ (6.5mm) needles, with RS facing, pick up and knit (see page 124) 24 sts across cast-on edge of hat between markers.
Row 1: Purl.
Row 2: K2, k2tog, k to last 4 sts, ssk, k2. *(22 sts)*
Row 3: Purl.
Rep rows 2–3 once more. *(20 sts)*
Row 6: K2, k2tog, k to last 4 sts, ssk, k2. *(18 sts)*
Row 7: P2tog, p to last 2 sts, p2tog. *(16 sts)*
Rep rows 6–7 once more. *(12 sts)*
Row 10: K2, m1, k to last 2 sts, m1, k2. *(14 sts)*
Row 11: P2, m1, p to last 2 sts, m1, p2. *(16 sts)*
Rep rows 10–11 once more. *(20 sts)*
Row 14: K2, m1, k to last 2 sts, m1, k2. *(22 sts)*
Row 15: Purl.
Rep rows 14–15 once more. *(24 sts)*
Bind (cast) off.

To make up

Sew the back seam using flat stitch (see page 125). Fold the peak forward so that the right sides of the peak top and bottom are facing each other. Oversew the side seams and turn the peak the right way out. Using the template on page 114, cut the peak shape from paper then, if necessary, enlarge or reduce it to the right size for your knitted peak. The peak should fit snuggly over the shape. Draw round the template and cut the final shape from the clear plastic. Put the plastic piece inside the peak and slip stitch along the inside edge of the peak to secure. Weave in all loose ends.

TURBAN-STYLE BEANIE

*If you're looking for a touch of
1940s glamour, this turban-style
beanie—which is so much easier
to knit than you'd think at first
glance—is the answer to your
wishes. If you've never worked in
reverse stockinette (stocking) stitch
before, don't panic; it's only what's
usually called the "wrong side"
of stockinette (stocking) stitch. I
knitted this turban in a delicate eau-
de-nil shade, which I felt reflected
the vintage look nicely, but it would
also work beautifully in super-bright
shades. And for a bit of added chic,
pin a vintage gem to the band.*

Yarn
Rowan Pure Wool Worsted (100%
wool) worsted (Aran) yarn
1 x 3½oz (100g) ball (219yd/200m) in
shade 137 Oxygen

Needles and equipment
US 7 (4.5mm) knitting needles
Yarn sewing needle

Gauge (tension)
20 sts and 25 rows in stockinette
(stocking) stitch to a 4-in (10-cm)
square on US 7 (4.5mm) needles.

Measurements
The finished hat measures approx.
20in (50cm) circumference and 7½in
(19cm) high.

Abbreviations
See page 126.

For the turban
Cast on 102 sts.
Beg with a p row (RS), work 7 rows in
rev st st.
Beg with a p row, work 3 rows in st st.
Beg with a p row, work 5 rows in rev
st st.
Rep the last 8 rows, 3 times more.
Beg with a p row, work 11 rows in st st.
Row 51: K7, [sk2po, k14] 5 times,
sk2po, k7. *(90 sts)*
Row 52: Purl.
Row 53: K6, [sk2po, k12] 5 times,
sk2po, k6. *(78 sts)*
Row 54: Purl.
Row 55: K5, [sk2po, k10] 5 times,
sk2po, k5. *(66 sts)*
Row 56: Purl.
Row 57: K4, [sk2po, k8] 5 times,
sk2po, k4. *(54 sts)*
Row 58: Purl.
Row 59: K3, [sk2po, k6] 5 times,
sk2po, k3. *(42 sts)*
Row 60: Purl.

Row 61: K2, [sk2po, k4] 5 times,
sk2po, k2. *(30 sts)*
Row 62: Purl.
Row 63: K1, [sk2po, k2] 5 times,
sk2po, k1. *(18 sts)*
Row 64: [P2tog] to end. *(9 sts)*
Break yarn, thread it through rem sts,
and pull up securely.

For the turban band
Cast on 9 sts.
Beg with a k row, work 20 rows in st st.
Bind (cast) off.

To make up
Sew the back seam using mattress
stitch (see page 124).
With the RS facing out, oversew the top
short end of the turban band to the
center of the hat, just after the last row
of reverse stockinette (stocking) stitch.
Oversew the other end to the underside
of the hat, in the same place.
Weave in all loose ends.

THREE-COLOR BOBBLE HAT

Sometimes, only something classically simple will fit the bill. So here is a traditional bobble hat that you can customize to your own style. Knit it in two colors and add a bobble in another color—just like I have. Knit it totally plain. Or knit it in stripes. I've chosen a lovely cotton-rich yarn for this hat, so you can keep it to hand to ward off any cool spring breezes. And it's chunky, so it will knit up in just an evening or two.

Yarn

Rowan All Seasons Chunky (60% cotton, 40% acrylic) chunky yarn
1 x 3½oz (100g) ball (93yd/85m) in shade 609 Jetsam (A)
1 x 3½oz (100g) ball (93yd/85m) in shade 603 Drift (B)
1 x 3½oz (100g) ball (93yd/85m) in shade 611 Samphire (C)

Needles and equipment

US 10½ (6.5mm) knitting needles
Yarn sewing needle
A pompom maker to make 2¾in (7cm) pompoms, or two cardboard circles each measuring 2¾in (7cm) in diameter with a 1¼in (3cm) diameter hole in the center.

Gauge (tension)

14 sts and 16 rows in stockinette (stocking) stitch to a 4-in (10-cm) square on US 10½ (6.5mm) needles.

Measurements

The finished hat measures approx. 10½in (50cm) circumference and 8¼in (21cm) high excluding the pompom.

Abbreviations

See page 126.

For the hat

Cast on 60 sts in A.
Row 1: [K2, p2] to end.
Rep row 1, 5 times more.
Break A and join in B.
Work 20 rows in st st beg with a k row.
Row 27: K4, [k2tog, k8] 5 times, k2tog, k4. *(54 sts)*
Row 28: Purl.
Row 29: K3, [sl2, k1, p2sso, k6] 5 times, sl2, k1, p2sso, k3.
Row 30: Purl.

Row 31: K2, [sl2, k1, p2sso, k4] 5 times, sl2, k1, p2sso, k2.
Row 32: Purl.
Row 33: K1, [sl2, k1, p2sso, k2] 5 times, sl2, k1, p2sso, k1.
Row 34: Purl.
Row 35: [Sl2, k1, p2sso] 6 times. Break yarn, thread it through rem sts, and pull up securely.

To make up

Sew the back seam using mattress stitch (see page 124).
Using the pompom maker or cardboard circles, make a pompom using C. Trim the pompom and use the tails of yarn to sew it to the top of the hat.
Weave in all loose ends.

FAIR ISLE BORDER BEANIE

A plain color beanie is all very well, but there are times when you'll want something with a little more panache—if only to show off your knitting skills. So if you're looking for your first foray into the world of stranded color knitting, this beanie with its classic Fair Isle border is a great first project. I've used a 100% wool light worsted (DK) yarn in a traditional scarlet and ecru, but if you want to go off-piste, the pattern would work well in lots of different color combinations.

Yarn
Debbie Bliss Rialto DK (100% wool) light worsted (DK) yarn
1 x 1¾oz (50g) ball (115yd/105m) in shade 012 Scarlet (A)
1 x 1¾oz (50g) ball (115yd/105m) in shade 002 Ecru (B)

Needles and equipment
US 6 (4mm) knitting needles
Yarn sewing needle

Gauge (tension)
22 sts and 30 rows in stockinette (stocking) stitch to a 4-in (10-cm) square on US 6 (4mm) needles.

Measurements
The finished hat measures approx. 16in (43cm) circumference and 7¾in (20cm) high. It should fit an average-size child of 9–12 years or a small adult.

Abbreviations
See page 126.

For the hat
Cast on 96 sts in A.
Row 1: [K2, p2] to end.
Rep row 1, 5 times more.
Beg with a k row, work 3 rows in st st.
Break A and join in B.
Row 10: Purl.
Leave B at side of work and join in A.
Row 11: Knit.
Row 12: Purl.
Rows 13–23: Work from chart, ending with a RS row.
Leave B at side of work and use A.
Row 24: Purl.

Row 25: Knit.
Break A and cont in B.
Row 26: Purl.
Break B and knit remainder of hat in A.
Beg with a k row, work 16 rows in st st.
Row 43: K7, [skpo, k14] 5 times, skpo, k7. *(90 sts)*
Row 44 and every alt row unless stated: Purl.
Row 45: K6, [sk2po, k12] 5 times, sk2po, k6. *(78 sts)*
Row 47: K5, [sk2po, k10] 5 times, sk2po, k5. *(66 sts)*
Row 49: K4, [sk2po, k8] 5 times, sk2po, k4. *(54 sts)*
Row 51: K3, [sk2po, k6] 5 times, sk2po, k3. *(42 sts)*
Row 53: K6, [sk2po, k4] 5 times, sk2po, k2. *(30 sts)*
Row 55: K6, [sk2po, k2] 5 times, sk2po, k1. *(18 sts)*
Row 56: [P2tog] to end. *(9 sts)*
Break yarn, thread it through rem sts, and pull up securely.

To make up
Sew the back seam using mattress stitch (see page 124).
Weave in all loose ends.

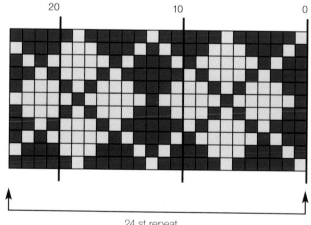

24 st repeat

key

Scarlet (A)

Ecru (B)

PUMPKIN BEANIE

Celebrate the Fall with a good-enough-to-eat pumpkin hat—an absolute essential for any Halloween party wardrobe. The hat is knitted in a lovely soft yarn with a touch of alpaca, and as I've used it double, you'll find the hat knits up really quickly. I've added a couple of small leaves and a curly tendril to mine—but you could always leave yours plain if you prefer.

Yarn

Bergere de France Chinaillon (56% acrylic, 30% wool, 10% alpaca, 4% viscose) light worsted (DK) yarn 2 x 1¾oz (50g) balls (153yd/140m) in shade 24508 Citrouille (A)

Patons Diploma Gold DK (55% wool, 25% acrylic, 29% nylon) light worsted (DK) yarn 1 x 1¾oz (50g) ball (131yd/120m) in shade 6125 Apple Green (B)

Needles and equipment

US 9 (5.5mm) knitting needles
US 6 (4mm) knitting needles
Yarn sewing needle

Gauge (tension)

12 sts and 14 rows in stockinette (stocking) stitch to a 4-in (10-cm) square on US 9 (5.5mm) needles, using yarn A doubled.

Measurements

The finished hat measures approx. 16in (40cm) circumference and 7in (18cm) high excluding stalk. It should fit an average-size child of 5–10 years.

Abbreviations

See page 126.

For the hat

Using US 9 (5.5mm) needles and A, cast on 63 sts using the yarn double.
Row 1: K3, [p1, k3] to end.
Row 2: K1, p1, [k3, p1] to last st, k1.
Rep rows 1–2, 9 times more.
Row 21: K2, [sl2, k1, p2sso, k2, p1, k2] to last 5 sts, sl2, k1, p2sso, k2. *(47 sts)*
Row 22: K1, [p1, k1, p1, k3] to last 4 sts, [p1, k1] twice.
Row 23: K4, [sl2, k1, p2sso, k3] to last st, k1. *(33 sts)*
Row 24: K1, [p1, k1] to end.
Row 25: K1, [k2togtbl] to end. *(17 sts)*
Row 26: [P2tog] to last st, p1. *(9 sts)*
Break A and join in B for the stalk, using the yarn double.
Beg with a k row, work 8 rows in st st.
Bind (cast) off.

Leaf

Make 2

The leaves are knitted from the tip to the base.

Using US 9 (5.5mm) needles and B, cast on 2 sts.
Row 1: Inc, k1. *(3 sts)*
Row 2: Purl.
Row 3: [Inc] twice, k1. *(5 sts)*
Row 4: Purl.
Row 5: Inc, k2, inc, k1. *(7 sts)*
Beg with a p row, work 5 rows in st st.
Row 11: K1, ssk, k1, k2tog, k1. *(5 sts)*
Row 12: P2tog, p1, p2tog. *(3 sts)*
Row 13: Sk2po. *(1 st)*
Break yarn and pull it through rem st.

Tendril

Make 1

Using US 6 (4mm) needles, cast on 40 sts in B, keeping your gauge (tension) loose.
Bind (cast) off tightly, so that the tendril twists naturally.

To make up

Sew the back seam of the main hat using flat stitch (see page 125) and the seam of the stalk using mattress stitch (see page 124), using matching yarns.
Sew the leaves and tendrils in place at the base of the stalk.
Weave in all loose ends.

HEART BEANIE

Pull the gently-rolled edge down to keep little ears cozy—or roll it up if you want a slightly more relaxed feel. This classic little beanie is a great project for knitters wanting to get to grips with knitting motifs, and is knitted entirely in stockinette (stocking) stitch. I've chosen a soft lavender and deep dusky pink—but the design would also work brilliantly in classic tones, such as scarlet and white, or navy and cream.

Yarn
Rowan Creative Focus Worsted (75% wool, 25% alpaca) worsted (Aran) yarn 1 x 3½oz (100g) ball (220yd/200m) in shade 0712 Lavender Heather (A)
Sirdar Snuggly DK (55% nylon, 45% acrylic) light worsted (DK) yarn 1 x 1¾oz (50g) ball (180yd/165m) in shade 420 Lolly (B)

Needles and equipment
US 7 (4.5mm) knitting needles
Yarn sewing needle

Gauge (tension)
20 sts and 24 rows in stockinette (stocking) stitch to a 4-in (10-cm) square on US 7 (4.5mm) needles.

Measurements
The finished hat measures approx. 16in (40cm) circumference and 18cm (7in) high. It should fit an average–size child of 5–10 years.

Abbreviations
See page 126.

For the hat
Before beginning your knitting, cut a 20-in (51-cm) length of A.
Cast on 73 sts in A from the main ball.
Beg with a k row, work 14 rows in st st.
Row 15: K36 in A, join B and k1, k in A to end.
Row 16: P35 in A, p3 in B, p in A (using the yarn end from the center of the ball) to end.
Row 17: K35 in A, k3 in B, k in A to end.
Row 18: P34 in A, p5 in B, p in A to end.
Row 19: K34 in A, k5 in B, k in A to end.
Row 20: P33 in A, p7 in B, p in A to end.
Row 21: K33 in A, k7 in B, k in A to end.
Row 22: P32 in A, p9 in B, p in A to end.
Row 23: K31 in A, k11 in B, k in A to end.
Row 24: P31 in A, p11 in B, p in A to end.

Row 25: K30 in A, k6 in B, k1 in A using cut length of yarn, k6 in B, k in A to end.
Row 26: P30 in A, p5 in B, p3 in A, p5 in B, p in A to end.
Row 27: K31 in A, k3 in B, k5 in A, k3 in B, k in A to end.
Cut B and the A coming from the outside of the ball of yarn.
Work remainder of hat in A only.
Beg with a p row, work 5 rows in st st.
Row 33: K5, [k2tog, k10] 3 times, k1, [k2tog, k10] twice, k2tog, k5. *(67 sts)*
Row 34: Purl.
Row 35: K4, [sk2po, k8] 3 times, k1, [sk2po, k8] twice, sk2po, k4. *(55 sts)*
Row 36: Purl.
Row 37: K3, [sk2po, k6] 3 times, k1, [sk2po, k6] twice, sk2po, k3. *(43 sts)*
Row 38: Purl.
Row 39: K2, [sk2po, k4] 3 times, k1, [sk2po, k4] twice, sk2po, k2. *(31 sts)*
Row 40: Purl.
Row 41: K1, [sk2po, k2] 3 times, k1, [sk2po, k2] twice, sk2po, k1. *(19 sts)*
Row 42: [P2tog] 9 times, p1. *(10 sts)*
Break yarn, thread it through rem sts, and pull up securely.

To make up
Sew the back seam using mattress stitch (see page 124).
Weave in all loose ends.

TRICOLOR BOBBLE HAT

If you're after a contemporary, nautical twist on the most classic of bobble hats, look no further. This striped hat with its distinctive red bobble is knitted in a baby-soft merino yarn in straightforward stockinette (stocking) stitch. It's simple enough to suit novice knitters and is an ideal project for those keen to dip their toes into the world of two-color knitting.

Yarn

Sublime Extra Fine Merino DK (100% extra fine merino wool) light worsted (DK) yarn
1 x 1¾oz (50g) ball (127yd/116m) in shade 015 Clipper (A)
1 x 1¾oz (50g) ball (127yd/116m) in shade 307 Julep (B)
1 x 1¾oz (50g) ball (127yd/116m) in shade 167 Red Hot (C)

Needles and equipment

US 5 (3.75mm) knitting needles
US 6 (4mm) knitting needles
Yarn sewing needle
A pompom maker to make 2¾in (7cm) pompoms, or two cardboard circles each measuring 2¾in (7cm) in diameter with a 1¼in (3cm) diameter hole in the center.

Gauge (tension)

22 sts and 28 rows in stockinette (stocking) stitch to a 4-in (10-cm) square on US 6 (4mm) needles.

Measurements

The finished hat measures approx. 15in (38cm) circumference and 8in (20cm) high, excluding pompom. It should fit an average-size child of 5–10 years.

Abbreviations

See page 126.

For the hat

Using US 5 (3.75mm) needles, cast on 102 sts in A.
Row 1: [K3, p3] to end.
Rep row 1, 13 times more.
Leave A at side, join in B and change to US 6 (4mm) needles.
Row 15: Knit.
Row 16: Purl.
Leave B at side and use A.
Row 17: Knit.
Row 18: Purl.
Rep rows 15–18, 7 times more.
Leave A at side and use B.
Row 47: K7, [sl2, k1, p2sso, k14] 5 times, sl2, k1, p2sso, k7. *(90 sts)*
Row 48: Purl.
Leave B at side and use A.
Row 49: K6, [sl2, k1, p2sso, k12] 5 times, sl2, k1, p2sso, k6. *(78 sts)*

Row 50: Purl.
Leave A at side and use B.
Row 51: K5, [sl2, k1, psso, k10] 5 times, sl2, k1, p2sso, k5. *(66 sts)*
Row 52: Purl.
Leave B at side and use A.
Row 53: K4, [sl2, k1, psso, k8] 5 times, sl2, k1, p2sso, k4. *(54 sts)*
Row 54: Purl.
Leave A at side and use B.
Row 55: K3, [sl2, k1, p2sso, k6] 5 times, sl2, k1, p2sso, k3. *(42 sts)*
Row 56: Purl.
Leave B at side and use A.
Row 57: K2, [sl2, k1, p2sso, k4] 5 times, sl2, k1, p2sso, k2. *(30 sts)*
Row 58: Purl.
Break A and use B.
Row 59: K1, [sl2, k1, p2sso, k2] 5 times, sl2, k1, p2sso, k1. *(18 sts)*
Row 60: [P2tog] to end. *(9 sts)*
Break yarn, thread it through rem sts, and pull up securely.

To make up

Sew the back seam using mattress stitch (see page 124).
Using the pompom maker or cardboard circles, make a pompom in C. Trim the pompom and use the tails of yarn to sew it to the top of the hat.
Weave in all loose ends.

BOW BEANIE

Pretty as a picture, this 1920s-inspired hat is made from a cotton mix yarn—so it's the ideal head warmer for those early days of spring, when you don't need something too warm and fuzzy. The yarn is available in a range of pretty sherbet shades—I've chosen pale green and the palest of yellows, but you can create your beanie in any shade you want. And if you're after something just a little less girly, simply omit the bow. The hat is worked exclusively in knit and purl stitches, so is an ideal early project for the new knitter—but I've got a feeling it's going to be a hit for experienced knitters, too.

Yarn
Lion Brand Baby's First (55% acrylic, 45% cotton) chunky yarn
1 x 3½oz (100g) ball (120yd/110m) in shade 156 Beanstalk (A)
1 x 3½oz (100g) ball (120yd/110m) in shade 099 Pixie Dust (B)

Needles and equipment
US 10 (6mm) knitting needles
Yarn sewing needle

Gauge (tension)
12 sts and 18 rows in stockinette (stocking) stitch to a 4-in (10-cm) square on US 10 (6mm) needles.

Measurements
The finished hat measures approx. 16½in (42cm) circumference and 7½in (19cm) high. It should fit an average-size child of 5–10 years.

Abbreviations
See page 126.

For the hat
Cast on 60 sts in A.
Row 1: [K2, p2] to end.
Rep row 1, 3 times more.
Row 5: Knit.
Row 6: Purl.
Leave A at side and join in B.
Beg with a k row, work 4 rows in st st.
Break B and work remainder of main hat in A.
Beg with a k row, work 14 rows in st st.
Row 25: K4, [k2tog, k8] 5 times, k2tog, k4. *(54 sts)*
Row 26: Purl.
Row 27: K3, [sl2, k1, p2sso, k6] 5 times, sl2, k1, p2sso, k3. *(42 sts)*

Row 28: Purl.
Row 29: K2, [sl2, k1, p2sso, k4] 5 times, sl2, k1, p2sso, k2. *(30 sts)*
Row 30: Purl.
Row 31: K1, [sl2, k1, p2sso, k2] 5 times, sl2, k1, p2sso, k1. *(18 sts)*
Row 32: [P2tog] to end. *(9 sts)*
Row 31: [K2tog] twice, k1, [ssk] twice. *(5 sts)*
Break yarn, thread it through rem sts, and pull up securely.

For the bow main part
Cast on 9 sts in B.
Beg with a k row, work 20 rows in st st.
Bind (cast) off.

For the bow center
Cast on 3 sts in B.
Beg with a k row, work 6 rows in st st.
Bind (cast) off.

To make up
Sew the back seam using flat stitch (see page 125).
Wrap the bow center around the middle of the bow, remembering that the front side of the bow is the "reverse" side of the stockinette (stocking) stitch. Sew the bow in place on the center of the band on the hat.
Weave in all loose ends.

KNITTED CROWN

Transform the child in your life into a prince or princess with this cute knitted crown. I've gone down the traditional route and knitted mine in a soft gold yarn—but choose any color you like. I've kept to a clean, simple look—as I thought the lacy stitch was quite fancy enough, but if you want a burst of added bling, sew on a few sequins and gems, or whatever you can find in your craft box.

Yarn

Lion Brand Hometown USA (100% acrylic) super-chunky yarn
1 x 5oz (142g) ball (81yd/74m) in shade 170 Las Vegas Gold
1¼yd/1m gold jewelry wire (optional, but not suggested if the crown is for a very young child)

Needles and equipment

US 10 (6mm) knitting needles
Yarn sewing needle

Gauge (tension)

11 sts and 16 rows in stockinette (stocking) stitch to a 4-in (10-cm) square on US 10 (6mm) needles.

Measurements

The finished crown measures approx. 16in (40cm) circumference and 4¼in (11cm) high. It should fit an average-size child of 4–6 years.

Abbreviations

See page 126.

For the crown

Cast on 4 sts.
Row 1: K1, yo, k1, p1, k1. *(5 sts)*
Row 2 and every WS row: K2, p to end.
Row 3: K1, yo, k2, p1, k1. *(6 sts)*
Row 5: K1, yo, k1, k2tog, yo, p1, k1. *(7 sts)*
Row 7: K1, yo, k1, k2tog, yo, k1, p1, k1. *(8 sts)*
Row 9: K1, yo, k1, k2tog, yo, k2, p1, k1. *(9 sts)*
Row 11: K1, yo, [k1, k2tog, yo] twice, p1, k1. *(10 sts)*
Row 13: Cast (bind) off 6 sts, yo, k1, p1, k1. *(5 sts)*
Rep rows 2–13, 5 times more.
Bind (cast) off rem sts, working in stitch patt.

With RS facing, pick up and knit 40 sts evenly along the lower edge.
Knit 2 rows.
Bind (cast) off.

To make up

Sew the back seam using flat stitch (see page 125).
Weave in all loose ends.
Using the needle, thread the wire through the top of the peaks of the crown.

Template

This template is for the Peaked Newsboy Beret (pattern on page 105). The template is full size, but follow the instructions in the pattern, and reduce or enlarge the size as necessary to fit your own knitted peak.

Techniques

In this section you'll find basic knitting techniques that will let you make most of the hats in this book. You can substitute the yarn recommended in a pattern with the same weight of yarn in a different brand, but you will need to check the gauge (tension). When calculating the quantity of yarn you require, it is the length of yarn in each ball that you need to check, rather than the weight of the ball; the length of yarn per ball in each recommended project yarn is given in the pattern.

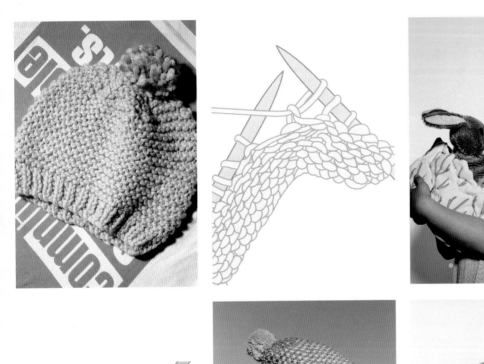

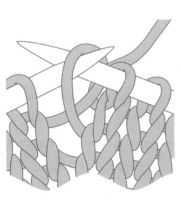

Gauge (tension)

A gauge (tension) is given with each pattern to help you make your hat the same size as the sample. The gauge is given as the number of stitches and rows you need to work to produce a 4-in (10-cm) square of knitting.

Using the recommended yarn and needles, cast on 8 stitches more than the gauge (tension) instruction asks for—so if you need to have 10 stitches to 4in (10cm), cast on 18 stitches. Working in pattern as instructed, work eight rows more than is needed. Bind (cast) off loosely.

Lay the swatch flat without stretching it. Lay a ruler across the stitches as shown, with the 2in (5cm) mark centered on the knitting, then put a pin in the knitting at the start of the ruler and at the 4in (10cm) mark: the pins should be well away from the edges of the swatch. Count the number of stitches between the pins. Repeat the process across the rows to count the number of rows to 4in (10cm).

If the number of stitches and rows you've counted is the same as the number asked for in the instructions, you have the correct gauge (tension). If you do not have the same number then you will need to change your gauge (tension).

To change gauge (tension) you need to change the size of your knitting needles. A good rule of thumb to follow is that one difference in needle size will create a difference of one stitch in the gauge (tension). You will need to use larger needles to achieve fewer stitches and smaller ones to achieve more stitches.

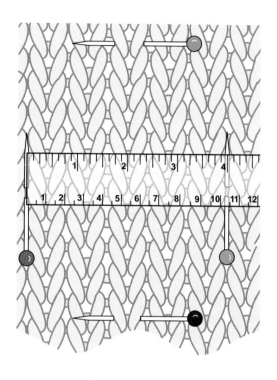

Soak and shape

Some of the hats will need soaking and easing into the finished shape in order to look their best. This also helps smooth out any uneven stitches. Soak the hat in lukewarm water, then squeeze out as much of the water as you can—but don't be tempted to wring-out the hat, as that will pull it out of shape. Then gently ease the hat into the final shape and place on a horizontal rack to dry naturally.

Holding needles

If you are a knitting novice, you will need to discover which is the most comfortable way for you to hold your needles.

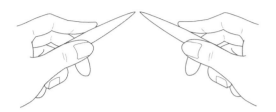

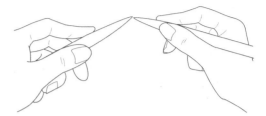

Like a knife

Pick up the needles, one in each hand, as if you were holding a knife and fork—that is to say, with your hands lightly over the top of each needle. As you knit, you will tuck the blunt end of the right-hand needle under your arm, let go with your hand and use your hand to manipulate the yarn, returning your hand to the needle to move the stitches along.

Like a pen

Now try changing the right hand so you are holding the needle as you would hold a pen, with your thumb and forefinger lightly gripping the needle close to its pointed tip and the shaft resting in the crook of your thumb. As you knit, you will not need to let go of the needle but simply slide your right hand forward to manipulate the yarn.

Holding yarn

As you knit, you will be working stitches off the left needle and onto the right needle, and the yarn you are working with needs to be tensioned and manipulated to produce an even fabric. To hold and tension the yarn you can use either your right or left hand. Try both methods to discover which works best for you.

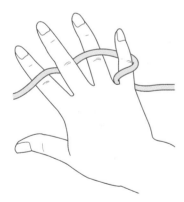

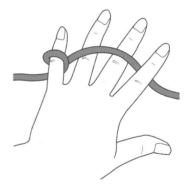

Yarn in right hand

With the ball of yarn on the right, catch the yarn around your little finger then lace it over the third finger, under the middle finger, and over the first finger of your right hand.

Yarn in left hand

With the ball of yarn on your left, catch the yarn around your little finger then take it over the third and middle fingers. Most left-handed knitters will also find that, even if they reverse the direction of knitting (working stitches off the right needle onto the left needle), using the left hand to manipulate the yarn will be easier to manage. To knit and purl in the Continental style (see pages 119 and 120), hold the yarn in your left hand.

Making a slip knot

You will need to make a slip knot to form your first cast-on stitch.

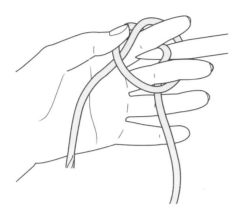

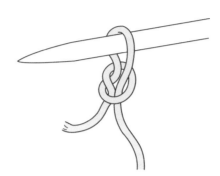

1 With the ball of yarn on your right, lay the end of the yarn on the palm of your left hand and hold it in place with your left thumb. With your right hand, take the yarn round your top two fingers to form a loop. Take the knitting needle through the back of the loop from right to left and use it to pick up the strand nearest to the yarn ball, as shown in the diagram. Pull the strand through to form a loop at the front.

2 Slip the yarn off your fingers leaving the loop on the needle. Gently pull on both yarn ends to tighten the knot. Then pull on the yarn leading to the ball of yarn to tighten the knot on the needle.

Casting on (cable method)

There are a few methods of casting on but the one used for the projects in this book is the cable method, which uses two needles.

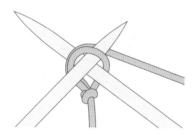

1 Make a slip knot as shown above. Put the needle with the slip knot into your left hand. Insert the point of your other needle into the front of the slip knot and under the left needle. Wind the yarn from the ball of yarn around the tip of the right needle.

2 Using the tip of your needle, draw the yarn through the slip knot to form a loop. This loop is your new stitch. Slip the loop from the right needle onto the left needle.

3 To make the next stitch, insert the tip of your right needle between the two stitches. Wind the yarn over the right needle, from left to right, then draw the yarn through to form a loop. Transfer this loop to your left needle. Repeat until you have cast on the right number of stitches for your project.

Basic stitches

Most people in the English-speaking world knit using a method called English (or American) knitting. However, in parts of Europe, people prefer a method known as Continental knitting. If you are new to knitting, try both techniques to see which works better for you.

Making a knit stitch

1 Hold the needle with the cast-on stitches in your left hand, and then insert the point of the right needle into the front of the first stitch from left to right. Wind the yarn around the point of the right needle, from left to right.

2 With the tip of your right needle, pull the yarn through the stitch to form a loop. This loop is your new stitch.

3 Slip the original stitch off the left needle by gently pulling your right needle to the right. Repeat these steps till you have knitted all the stitches on your left needle. To work the next row, transfer the needle with all the stitches into your left hand.

Making a knit stitch Continental style

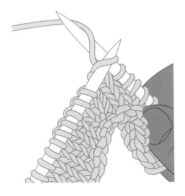

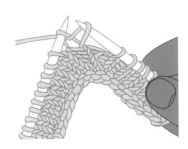

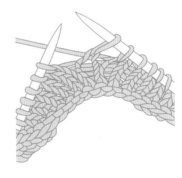

1 Hold the needle with the stitches to be knitted in your left hand, and then insert the tip of the right needle into the front of the first stitch from left to right. Holding the yarn fairly taut with your left hand at the back of your work, use the tip of your right needle to pick up a loop of yarn.

2 With the tip of your right needle, bring the yarn through the original stitch to form a loop. This loop is your new stitch.

3 Slip the original stitch off the left needle by gently pulling your right needle to the right. Repeat these steps till you have knitted all the stitches on your left needle. To work the next row, transfer the needle with all the stitches into your left hand.

Making a purl stitch

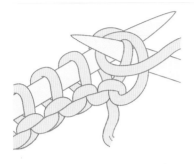  

1 Hold the needle with the stitches in your left hand, and then insert the point of the right needle into the front of the first stitch from right to left. Wind the yarn around the point of the right needle, from right to left.

2 With the tip of the right needle, pull the yarn through the stitch to form a loop. This loop is your new stitch.

3 Slip the original stitch off the left needle by gently pulling your right needle to the right. Repeat these steps till you have purled all the stitches on your left needle. To work the next row, transfer the needle with all the stitches into your left hand.

Making a purl stitch Continental style

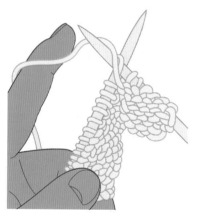 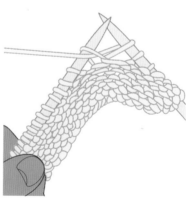 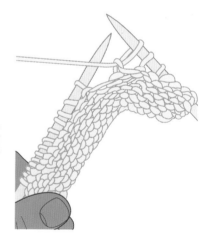

1 Hold the needle with the stitches to be knitted in your left hand, and then insert the tip of the right needle into the front of the first stitch from right to left. Holding the yarn fairly taut at the front of your work, use the tip of your right needle to pick up a loop of yarn.

2 With the tip of your right needle, bring the yarn through the original stitch to form a loop.

3 Slip the original stitch off the left needle by gently pulling your right needle to the right. Repeat these steps till you have purled all the stitches on your left needle. To work the next row, transfer the needle with all the stitches into your left hand.

Binding (casting) off

You need to bind (cast) off your stitches to complete the projects and stop the knitting unraveling.

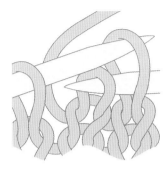

1 First knit two stitches in the normal way. With the point of your left needle, pick up the first stitch you have just knitted and lift it over the second stitch. Knit another stitch so that there are two stitches on your needle again. Repeat the process of lifting the first stitch over the second stitch. Continue this process until there is just one stitch remaining on the right needle.

2 Break the yarn, leaving a tail of yarn long enough to stitch your work together. Pull the tail all the way through the last stitch. Slip the stitch off the needle and pull it fairly tightly to make sure it is secure.

Increasing

There are two methods of increasing used in this book.

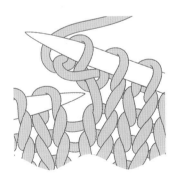

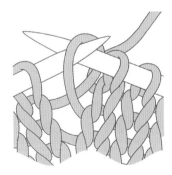

Increase (inc)

Start knitting your stitch in the normal way but instead of slipping the "old" stitch off the needle, knit into the back of it and then slip the "old" stitch off the needle in the normal way. The same principle is used to increase on a purl row, except that you purl the stitches instead of knitting them.

Make one (m1)

Pick up the horizontal strand between two stitches on your left-hand needle. Knit into the back of the loop and transfer the stitch to the right-hand needle in the normal way. (It is important to knit into the back of the loop so that the yarn is twisted and does not form a hole in your work.)

Decreasing

There are three different ways of decreasing used in this book.

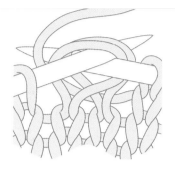

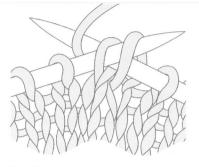

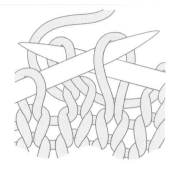

Knit two together (k2tog)

This is the simplest way of decreasing. Simply insert your needle through two stitches instead of the normal one when you begin your stitch and then knit them in the normal way.

The same principle is used to decrease on a purl row, except that you purl the stitches together instead of knitting them.

Slip, slip, knit (ssk)

Slip one stitch knitwise, and then the next stitch knitwise onto your right-hand needle, without knitting them. Then insert the left-hand needle from left to right through the front loops of both the slipped stitches and knit them as normal.

Slip one, knit one, pass the slipped stitch over (skpo)

Slip the first stitch knitwise from the left to the right needle without knitting it. Knit the next stitch. Then lift the slipped stitch over the knitted stitch and drop it off the needle.

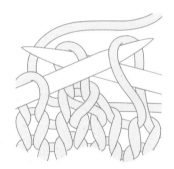

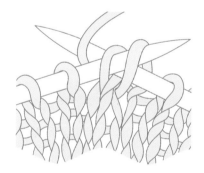

Slip one, knit two together, pass the slipped stitch over (sk2po)

Slip the first stitch knitwise from the left to the right needle without knitting it. Knit the next two stitches together (see k2tog, above). Then lift the slipped stitch over the knitted stitch and drop it off the needle.

Slip two stitches, knit the next stitch, then pass the slipped stitches over (sl2, k1, p2sso)

Slip one stitch knitwise, and then the next stitch knitwise onto your right-hand needle, without knitting them. Then knit the next stitch. Then insert the left-hand needle from left to right through the front loops of both the slipped stitches and lift them over the knitted stitch and drop them off the needle.

Cables

These involve moving groups of stitches, and you will need a cable needle to hold the stitches being moved. Work a six-stitch cable as shown here: if it is a four stitch cable, then slip two stitches onto the needle and knit two, rather than three. For an eight-stitch cable, slip four stitches onto the needle and knit four.

A six-stitch front cable (c6f)

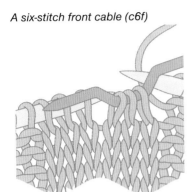 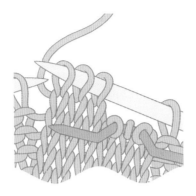 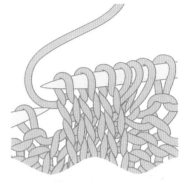

1 Work to the position of the cable. Slip the next three stitches on the left-hand needle onto the cable needle, keeping the cable needle in front of the work. Leave the three stitches on the cable needle in the middle so they don't slip off.

2 Knit the next three stitches off the left-hand needle in the usual way.

3 Then knit the three stitches off the cable needle and the cable is completed.

A six-stitch back cable (c6b)

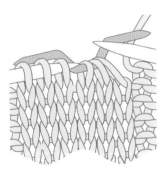 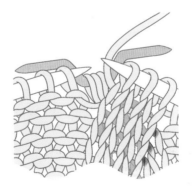 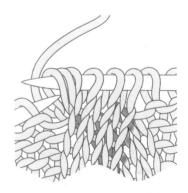

1 Work to the position of the cable. Slip the next three stitches on the left-hand needle onto the cable needle, keeping the cable needle at the back of the work. Leave the three stitches in the middle of the cable needle so they don't slip off.

2 Knit the next three stitches off the left-hand needle in the usual way.

3 Then knit the three stitches off the cable needle and the cable is completed.

Picking up stitches

For some projects, you will need to pick up stitches along either a horizontal edge (the cast-on or bound-/cast-off edge of your knitting), or a vertical edge (the edges of your rows of knitting).

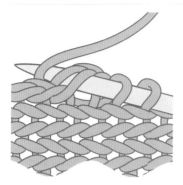

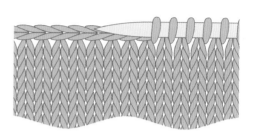

Along a vertical edge

With the right side of the knitting facing you, insert a knitting needle from the front to back between the first and second stitches of the first row. Wind the yarn around the needle and pull through a loop to form the new stitch. Normally you have more gaps between rows than stitches you need to pick up and knit. To make sure your picking up is even, you will have to miss a gap every few rows.

Along a horizontal edge

This is worked in the same way as picking up stitches along a vertical edge, except that you will work through the cast-on stitches rather than the gaps between rows. You will normally have the same number of stitches to pick up and knit as there are existing stitches.

Mattress stitch

There are two versions of this stitch—one used to join two vertical edges and the other used to join two horizontal edges.

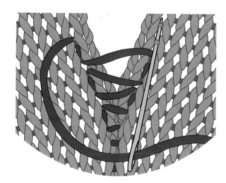

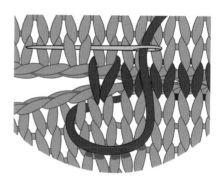

Vertical edges

Place the two edges side by side with the right side facing you. Take a yarn sewing needle under the running thread between the first two stitches of one side, then under the corresponding running thread of the other side. Pull your yarn up fairly firmly every few stitches.

Horizontal edges

Place the two edges side by side with the right side facing you. Take a yarn sewing needle under the two "legs" of the last row of stitches on the first piece of knitting. Then take your needle under the two "legs" of the corresponding stitch on the second piece of knitting. Pull your yarn up fairly firmly every few stitches.

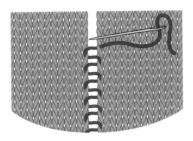

Flat stitch

Unlike mattress stitch, this stitch creates a join that is completely flat. Lay the two edges to be joined side by side with the right side facing you. Using a yarn sewing needle, pick up the very outermost strand of knitting from one side and then the other, working your way along the seam and pulling your yarn up firmly every few stitches.

Sewing in ends

The easiest way to finish yarn ends is to run a few small stitches forward then backward through your work, ideally in a seam. It is a good idea to use a yarn sewing needle to do this and take the tail between the strands that make up your yarn, as this will help make sure the tail stays in place.

Crochet techniques

While the hats in this book are all knitted rather than crocheted, for the Fairytale Hood (see pages 18 and 82) you will need to know how to work a simple crochet edging.

Crochet edging

A crochet edging can be worked along a horizontal edge or a vertical edge, but the basic technique is the same.

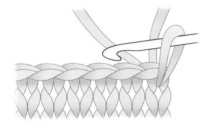

1 Insert the crochet hook in the first space between stitches. Wind the yarn round the hook and pull a loop of yarn through.

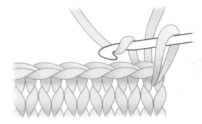

2 Wind the yarn round the hook again and then pull the loop through to make a single chain.

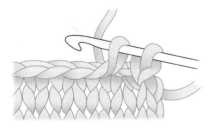

3 Insert the hook through the next stitch, wind the yarn round the hook, and pull through a second loop of yarn.

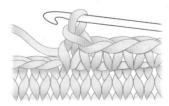

4 Wind the yarn round the hook and pull a loop of yarn through both loops on the hook. Repeat steps 3 and 4, inserting the hook into the spaces between stitches in an even pattern.

For crochet edging along a vertical edge, insert your hook into the spaces between the edges of the rows rather than the spaces between stitches.

Abbreviations

beg	begin(ning)
C6(8:12)B	cable six (eight:twelve) back: see page 123
C6F	cable six front: see page 123
cm	centimeter(s)
cont	continue
g	gram(s)
in	inch(es)
inc	increase, by working into front and back of next stitch: see page 121
k	knit
k2tog	knit two stitches together, to decrease: see page 122
kwise	purlwise, slip a stitch as if you were going to knit it
m1	make one stitch, by knitting into the strand between two stitches, to increase: see page 121
m	meter(s)
mm	millimeter
oz	ounces
p	purl
p2tog	purl two stitches together, to decrease: see page 122
psso	pass slipped stitch over, pass a slipped stitch over another stitch
p2sso	pass two slipped stitches over, pass two slipped stitches over another stitch
pwise	purlwise, slip a stitch as if you were going to purl it
rem	remain(ing)
rep	repeat
RS	right side
RT	right twist: knit into the second stitch from the tip of the left-hand needle, but don't pull the stitch off the needle. Then knit into the first stitch on the left-hand needle and slip both stitches off the needle together.
skpo	slip one stitch, knit one stitch, pass slipped stitch over knitted one, to decrease: see page 122
sk2po	slip one stitch, knit two together, pass slipped stitch over knitted one, to decrease: see page 122
sl1(2)	slip one (two) stitch(es), from the left-hand needle to the right-hand needle without knitting it (them)
ssk	slip one stitch, slip one stitch, knit slipped stitches together, to decrease: see page 122
st(s)	stitch(es)
st st	stockinette (stocking) stitch
tbl	through the back loop, knit or purl though the back of the stitch
WS	wrong side
WT	with yarn at the back, slip the next stitch purlwise from the left-hand to the right-hand needle. Bring the yarn forward between the needles. Slip the stitch from the right-hand needle back to the left-hand needle. Take the yarn back between the needles. Turn the work.
yb	yarn back, between the tips of the needles
yd	yard(s)
yf	yarn forward, between the tips of the needles
yo	yarnover, wrap yarn around needle between stitches, to increase and to make an eyelet
[ ]	work instructions within square brackets as directed
*	work instructions after/between asterisk(s) as directed

Author's acknowledgments

My thanks to Cindy Richards, Penny Craig, Fahema Khanam, and everyone at CICO Books for their ideas and support. Thanks also to Kate Haxell, my editor, and Marilyn Wilson, the pattern checker, Terry Benson, the photographer, and Luis Peral, the stylist. I would also like to thank my sister, Louise Turner, for help with knitting, and my husband Roger Dromard and our son Louis, for letting me try the half-completed hats on them so I could work out the fit.

Publisher's acknowledgments

The publishers would like to thank the following company for lending goods for photography:

Oliver Bonas
147–148 Upper Street
London N1 1RA
www.oliverbonas.com

INDEX

SUPPLIERS

USA

Bergere de France
www.bergeredefrance.com
Website gives details of local US
suppliers

Knitting Fever Inc.
PO Box 336
315 Bayview Avenue
Amityville
NY 11701
Tel: +1 516 546 3600
www.knittingfever.com
Debbie Bliss, Katia, Sirdar, Sublime

Lion Brand Yarns
Tel: +800 258 YARN (9276)
Online sales and store locator on
website
www.lionbrand.com

Westminster Fibers
165 Ledge Street
Nashua
NH 03060
Tel: +800 445 9276
www.westminsterfibers.com
Rowan

Canada

Bergere de France
Tel: +1 800 361 0090
www.bergeredefrance.ca
Website gives details of local Canada
suppliers

Diamond Yarn
155 Martin Ross Unit 3
Toronto, ON
M3J 2L9
Tel: +1 416 736 6111
www.diamondyarn.com
Debbie Bliss, Katia, Sirdar, Sublime

Westminster Fibers
10 Roybridge Gate, Suite 200
Vaughan, ON
L4H 3MB
Tel: +800 263 2354
www.westminsterfibers.com
Rowan

UK

Bergere de France
www.bergeredefrance.co.uk
Website gives details of local suppliers
in the UK

Deramores
Online store only
Tel: 0800 488 0708
www.deramores.com
*Bergere de France, Cascade, Lion
Brand, Patons, Phildar, Rowan, Sublime*

John Lewis
Retail stores and online
www.johnlewis.com
Telephone numbers of local stores on
website
Tel: 03456 049049
Debbie Bliss, Patons, Rowan, Sirdar

Katia Yarns
Barcelona, Spain
Tel: +34 93 828 38 19
www.katia.com
Website gives details of local suppliers
in the UK.

Laughing Hens
Online store only
Tel: +44 (0) 1829 740903
www.laughing hens.com
*Bergere de France, Cascade, Debbie
Bliss, Rowan, Sublime*

Mavis Crafts
Online and retail store
Tel: +44 (0) 208 950 5445
www.mavis-crafts.com
Katia, Sirdar, Sublime

Rowan
Rowan Yarns
Green Lane Mill
Holmfirth
West Yorkshire HD9 2DX
Tel: +44 (0) 1484 681881
www.knitrowan.com

Sirdar
Sirdar Spinning Ltd
Flanshaw Lane
Wakefield
West Yorkshire WF2 9ND
Tel: +44 (0) 1924 231682
www.sirdar.co.uk

Australia

Black Sheep Wool 'n' Wares
www.blacksheepwool.com.au
*Debbie Bliss, Katia, Patons, Sirdar,
Sublime*

Prestige Yarns Pty Ltd
PO Box 39
Bulli
NSW 2516
Tel: +61 (0)2 4285 6669
www.prestigeyarns.com.au
Debbie Bliss

Rowan
www.knitrowan.com
Online store locator

Sun Spun
185 Canterbury Road
Canterbury
Victoria
VIC 3126
Tel: +61 (0)3 9830 1609
Debbie Bliss, Rowan, Sublime

Texyarns International PTY Ltd
P.O. Box 599
South Yarra
Victoria
VIC 3141
Tel: +61 (0)3 9427 9009
www.texyarns.com
Katia